VOLUME ONE

Who DO YOU THINK? You Are?

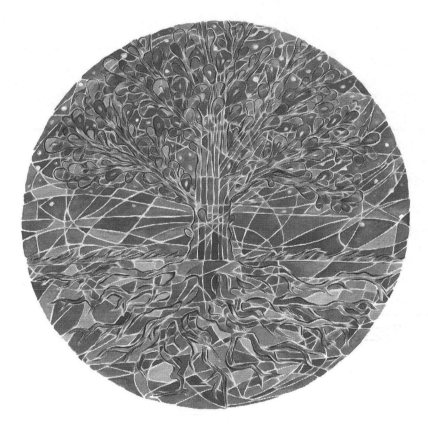

AN IN-DEPTH STUDY OF YOUR IDENTITY IN CHRIST

RAY LEIGHT

Who Do You Think You Are? Volume One: An In-Depth Study Of Your Identity In Christ
Copyright © 2015 by Raymond Leight

Requests for information should be addressed to: info@obedienceofbelief.org

Cover Design: Robert Schwendenmann, bobbyhere.com
Cover Art: Kyle Williams, kylewilliamsart.org
Interior Layout and Formatting: Robert Schwendenmann
Editors: Ashley Read, Julie Mustard, Melissa Amato

ISBN-10: 0-9966989-0-6
ISBN-13: 978-0-9966989-0-0

VOLUME ONE

AN IN-DEPTH STUDY OF YOUR IDENTITY IN CHRIST

This is Volume One of a two-volume set. The "Who Do You Think You Are?" set is a portion of the *Obedience of Belief*™ series. In Volume One, we will explore the truth of our redeemed, alive, righteous, fruitful, pure, and accepted identity in Christ. In Volume Two, we will explore the truth of our loved, known, trusted, pleasing, powerful, and purposeful identity in Christ.

TABLE OF CONTENTS

DEDICATION

I don't know what I would do without my family. My wife Kathryn, my daughter Rachel, and my son Riley are the core inspiration behind this book and the reasons this book is even possible.

Kathryn, I cannot even comprehend the ways that you have changed and impacted my life for the better. You are my best friend and my greatest encouragement. Your love, acceptance, and faith in me are priceless. Your help on this project is immeasurable. I couldn't have pulled this off without your help editing, clarifying, questioning, inspiring, and challenging me to dream. Look at what we have done together. I love you!

Rachel, I don't think I would still be alive if you hadn't entered into my life. I love you so much. It has been such a blessing to watch you grow into the powerful woman you are. To see God create you was the beginning of me even believing in Him—He so richly blessed me with you. You are one of the core inspirations for my faith. I am incredibly proud of you, and I am so glad that you married Josh and brought him into our family. Josh, thank you for your friendship and encouragement, especially while I was writing this study. I appreciate you and how well you love my daughter. I can't wait to see what God does through you and Rachel.

Riley, what an amazing man you are. I truly love you and could not be prouder. You are such an inspiration of authenticity, maturity, creativity, compassion, love, and genius. You coming into my life taught me many lessons on the increase and abundance of God's love. It has been a wonderful, humbling, inspiring, and motivating experience to witness the strength of your individuality and watch you develop into the man that you are.

Kathryn, Rachel, and Riley, thank you for being fully yourselves. I could not thrive and be who I am without your love, influence, and encouragement in my life.

ACKNOWLEDGEMENTS

My family and friends in Annapolis, MD

I cannot express to you how much I love you and how grateful I am that we are doing life together. This study would probably never have happened if it wasn't for all the ways you loved me, and helped sharpen me. Thank you for everything.

Dawna De Silva and Teresa Liebscher

Thank you for paving the way before us and providing healing, direction, and opportunity.

Trip Sizemore

Thank you for introducing me to an intimate lifestyle of freedom and healing with Jesus.

Ron and Della Proctor

Thank you for your leadership, inspiration, and training for a lifestyle of living by faith.

All of our ministry partners through the years

Thank you so much for all of your prayers, encouragement, and support throughout our ministry. Your partnership has impacted thousands of people's lives and helped to make this study a reality.

David and Paula Wentz

My family and I are eternally grateful for you. Thank you for introducing us to the Gospel, the Spirit-filled life, and the Word of God. Your love and leadership nurtured our desire for the presence of God and a deep hunger for the Word. We love you and your family.

NOTE FROM THE AUTHOR

Welcome to Volume One of the "Who Do You Think You Are?" study!

Who do you think you are?

Does that question sting with accusation or explode with possibility?

This is your opportunity to discover the amazing truth of your identity in Christ.

This life-changing study will allow you to discover who you are, how to accept yourself, and what it looks like to live out the truth of who God created you to be.

On this journey, you will learn how God has redeemed you, purified you, made you righteous, and restored you to life. You will learn how He accepts you completely and empowers you to walk in the Spirit. You will be personally challenged to believe the Scriptures and accept who God says you are.

This study can be done individually, in a one-on-one mentoring relationship, or shared together in a group setting.

May you be blessed in all the fullness of God as you go on this journey of discovering your true identity in Christ.

HOW TO EXPERIENCE THIS STUDY

The Scriptures in this study are from the ESV Bible translation unless otherwise noted. This study is best suited for an ESV translation, although it also works well with the NKJV, NASB, and the NIV.

Each session in this study includes several sections:

- *Scripture Study*

- *Consider This*

- *Statements of Faith*

- *The Restoration Process*

- *Identity Review*

- *Wrap Up*

- *Practical Take Away Tips*

Here are examples of the different sections and how to experience them:

Scripture Study

There will be a recommended reading and then an opportunity for you to fill in the specifics from those Scriptures.

It is highly recommended that you read the entire section of Scripture before going back to the specifically highlighted verses and filling in the blanks.

Here is an example:

Read Galatians 2:19-21

Galatians 2:20

I have been _____ *crucified with Christ.* _____

It is _____ *no longer I who live, but Christ who lives in me.* _____

And the life I now live in the flesh _____ *I live by faith in the Son of God, who*

_____ *loved me and gave Himself for me.* _____

After the 'Scripture Study' in each section, there will be an opportunity to consider what God is revealing to you.

Consider this...

In this section, you will have the opportunity to pause for a moment, review the Scriptures, consider what God is revealing to you in those Scriptures, and then consider how that may affect your life now.

Here is an example:

What are the truths that God is revealing to you personally about these Scriptures?

_____ *Jesus really does love me. He lives in me and I am*

_____ *not who I used to be. I truly live when I live by*

_____ *faith in Jesus.* _____

Next, you will have an opportunity to consider how this may affect your life.

How could believing these truths affect your life?

_____ *Feeling loved and knowing that Jesus lives in me, I would be*

_____ *free to be happy, accepted, and capable to do what He created*

_____ *me to do. I wouldn't be limited by fear.* _____

After that, you will have an opportunity to consider some practical steps you can take to experience the things that have been revealed.

What are some practical steps you can take to experience these truths in your life?

I can start focusing on what I am really thinking and what I put my faith in.

The 'Consider This' process is that simple. Just let the Word of God speak to you through the Holy Spirit while you are reading, and then write that down. Next, let yourself think about how that would affect your life, your relationships, your career, your family, your community, your thinking, etc. Write down whatever God reveals to you. After considering the truth, and the effects, you can let God reveal practical steps that you can take to come into agreement with these. All of this is for your own personal growth. Let yourself think, dream, and express your heart. You are not being tested; there is no way to do this wrong.

At the end of the 'Consider This' process, you will have an opportunity to ask the Holy Spirit to empower these truths and make them more real in your life.

After each 'Consider This' process, there will be a 'Statement of Faith' available for you to review.

Statement of Faith

These statements will be a concentration of the Scriptures you have studied in that section and are meant for you to read out loud, reflect upon, and let God's truth and love pour into your heart through the Holy Spirit. This can be a very powerful time for you to come into agreement with Jesus and declare His truth over your life (2 Corinthians 4:13).

At the end of each session you will also have the opportunity to go through the 'Restoration Process.' This process is something that has been developed from years of personal ministry in discipleship, mentoring, pastoring, and inner healing.

Here is an example of that process:

The Restoration Process

The foundation of the 'Restoration Process' is faith.   A simple definition of faith is:

> *Believing and living the truth of God's Word through the power of the Holy Spirit.*

With that understanding of faith, you will process through the Scriptures and allow the Lord to reveal the truth, and whether or not you are believing and living that truth.

During this whole process, it is recommended that you draw near to God and invite Him to be present with you.   Let this be more than just an intellectual exercise and let yourself experience this with the Lord. God is everywhere (Psalm 139:7), He is always with us (Matthew 28:20), and where He is present, there is healing (Acts 10:38) and freedom (2 Corinthians 3:17).

We will look at a specific Scripture. For example:

> I have been crucified with Christ. It is no longer I who live, but Christ who lives in me. And the life I now live in the flesh I live by faith in the Son of God, who loved me and gave Himself for me. – Galatians 2:20

You will have the opportunity to reflect on the Scripture and ask the Holy Spirit to reveal the truth of what God is actually saying in that Scripture.

After that, you list the truth that He revealed to you:

I have been crucified with Christ.

Christ lives in me.

Jesus loves me.

Jesus gave His life for me.

It is that easy—just list the truth that is revealed to you.

Then you will review the Scripture one more time and ask the Lord to reveal to you what thoughts, feelings, or lies you are believing that are opposed to this Scripture.

The reality is, all of us struggle to believe the truth at some level. Let the Lord reveal to you the things that you may believe that do not line up with His Word. You are not being tested; this is for your own personal growth. Be honest and let the Lord reveal these to you.

List the lies that He revealed to you:

My sins are too much.

I am not loved.

I am still the same old person that I have always been.

Then, you will review this list and ask the Lord if there is anyone you need to forgive that may have taught you these lies or hurt you with these lies. Keep in mind that forgiveness is not about accusation. We forgive in the same way that the Lord forgave us, by His blood that was shed on the cross (Colossians 3:13). Forgiveness is releasing through the blood of Jesus by the power of the Holy Spirit. That is the only way to forgive. You do not need to understand why someone did what they did, nor do you need to stir up compassion about their own issues first.

As the Lord leads, you will have the opportunity to express forgiveness out loud. There is power in the spoken word (Genesis 1:3; John 15:3).

There will be examples to follow through the process:

"In Jesus' name, I choose to forgive _____ for 'teaching me' or 'hurting me' with the lie that_____."

Feel free to add anything you may wish to add.

One of the aspects of the 'Restoration Process' is repentance. A simple definition of repentance is to change your mind. The Word tells us to be transformed by the renewal of our minds (Romans 12:2). Repentance leads to the knowledge of truth and will help us come to our senses and escape from the snare of the enemy (2 Timothy 2:25-26).

You will have the opportunity to repent during this process by breaking agreement with and renouncing the lies you believe. You will also have the opportunity to come into agreement with the truth that the Lord leads you to, thus escaping from any snare of the enemy.

Now that you have forgiven, you can deal with the lies themselves. Since God revealed to you that these are lies, you can repent from believing the lies by breaking agreement and renouncing them out loud.

Again, you will have an example to follow:

"In Jesus' name, I break agreement and renounce the lie that_____."

Here, you will take a moment and let the Holy Spirit comfort you and restore you. Allow the Holy Spirit to minister to your heart.

Then you can ask, *"Lord, is there anything You want to give me in return for all the lies I have released to You?"* (Isaiah 61:3)

Again, let yourself receive. The Lord could show you something, you could think about something, remember something, or you could feel something. Remember, you are not being tested. This is simply for your own personal growth.

Be sensitive to what the Lord reveals and don't discount what you receive.

As you receive them, you can list them here:

Peace, understanding, freedom

I feel Him embrace me and comfort me.

He is reminding me that He died for me; He wanted to do that for me.

He is showing me the chains that He has removed from me.

An extremely important aspect in personal development and discipleship is the need to forgive yourself. Jesus has forgiven all your trespasses and sins. Forgiving yourself is merely coming into agreement with Him.

You will have the opportunity to come into agreement with Him and forgive yourself.

Example:

"Jesus, I come into agreement with You and I completely forgive myself for any way I believed those lies. I release all the lies and I forgive myself."

Rest here for a moment and enjoy the freedom!

This is where it gets fun. Review the Scripture again.

I have been crucified with Christ. It is no longer I who live, but Christ who lives in me. And the life I now live in the flesh I live by faith in the Son of God, who loved me and gave Himself for me. – Galatians 2:20

Ask the Lord:

"Now that I have renounced the lies and forgiven everyone, what are the promises and the truths available to me in this Scripture?"

Let Him reveal to you what promises are available in this Scripture. Do not discount anything He reveals. He may remind you of promises that are for all believers, as well as something personal and meaningful to you and your life.

Take your time here. Stay here for a few moments, reflect on the Scripture, and allow Him to reveal the truths, promises, and grace available to you.

List what He reveals to you:

I can live a life where Jesus is with me all the time.

I can trust Him.

It is Christ who lives in me.

When the LORD restored the fortunes of Zion, we were like those who dream. Then our mouth was filled with laughter, and our tongue with shouts of joy; then they said among the nations, "The LORD has done great things for them." The LORD has done great things for us; we are glad. – Psalm 126:1-3

This is where it really gets good. Let yourself dream and think about these truths and promises. Let the Holy Spirit reveal how they would affect your life if you believed them and lived them. What would your life look like—be like? How could it affect your relationships, attitude, career, family, etc.?

Don't be afraid to dream. Be of good courage and take that step. This process has the ability to help you experience freedom and be released into the purpose God has for you. Take the time to let yourself develop in this area. Start small if you have to and let it grow.

List the effects of those truths and promises below:

I can live a life where I am free to pursue my dreams.

Jesus is always with me and lives in me. He will help me do everything I need to do. I will never be alone.

I can live my life free from isolation and have real relationships and friendships.

The next step will give you an opportunity to see what practical steps you can take that would help you experience everything God has revealed.

What are some practical steps you can take to experience this in your life?

Choose relationship and emotional connection instead of isolation.

Think about and write down my dreams. Start prioritizing them and make a plan. Ask for help from people I trust.

After dreaming about the promises, you will have an opportunity to let yourself receive those promises and truths and ask the Holy Spirit to empower you, make them more real in your life, and help you fulfill those dreams.

Thank the Lord out loud and receive the truths and promises He has revealed to you.

We can't just try harder and make these things happen. The only way is for God to empower us and guide us.

"Thank You, Lord, for the truth that _____ and thank You for the promise(s) of _____. I receive them from You by faith and ask that You empower them through the Holy Spirit in my life."

Before moving on, you can write down any additional thoughts that you have now that you have had time to pray, dream, and receive from the Lord.

Remember, you are not being tested. This is for you and your growth. Let yourself be free during this process.

I never gave myself permission to dream with God before.

I can't wait to finish this study and experience all the new

freedom the Lord has for me.

This 'Restoration Process' has helped set many people free into the fullness of their identity, grow deeper in relationship with Jesus, and be released into their God-given purpose. This simple process of restoration and freedom can help you be free also. Let yourself be free (Galatians 5:1).

At the end of every session, there will be a list of all the ways the Lord has described you in the session.

Identity

These are some of the ways the Lord describes you, as we learned from this session. This is who the Lord declares that you are:

Crucified with Christ	Redeemed	Loved
Saved	Reconciled	Set Free

After reviewing the list of identity descriptions, you will have the opportunity to write down the ones that stand out and inspire you:

Crucified with Christ

Loved

Take a moment to pray and reflect on these descriptions and write down a statement of faith of your own:

I am truly loved. I was crucified with Christ,

He loves me and I can really live in Him through faith.

Declare this over yourself out loud.

After the 'Identity' section, you will have an opportunity to do a final wrap up of what you learned from the session.

Wrap Up

Ask God:

"What is the main thing You want me to learn from this session?"

God truly loves me. I am loved.

"How can this affect my life now?"

Knowing and believing that I am loved, and that my old self was crucified with Christ, will bring freedom in my heart and my mind.

"What are some practical steps I can take to experience this in my life?"

Remind myself that I am not the old self.
Remember and declare the truth of who God says I am when I am tempted by the lies of my old identity.

Take a few moments right now and thank God for what He revealed to you.

At the end of each session you will have some practical take away tips to help you continue to know, believe, and live out the truth of God's Word.

Practical Take Away Tips

Read through the identity descriptions, memorize them, and declare them over yourself.

Re-read and declare the statements of faith from this session, both the given statements and the one you created for yourself.

Remind yourself of the truths and promises that God revealed to you. Continue to dream and ask God to make them more real in your life.

Copy and use the blank Restoration Process on page 165 of the Appendix with the following Scriptures, or any Scriptures that God highlights to you.

- Romans 5:17

- Romans 6:4

<hr>

May you receive a greater understanding and acceptance of your identity in Christ and be blessed in all the fullness and richness of God's mercy.

Thank you for taking the time to invest in yourself and the world through this study.

Be blessed!

*O*nce you were not a people, but now you are God's people; once you had not received mercy, but now you have received mercy.

– 1 Peter 2:10

Session 1

Am I Redeemed?

CONTENTS

ARE YOU REDEEMED?

As believers, we have been crucified with Christ; it is no longer we who live, but Christ who lives in us. Who we were before we repented is not the same as who we are now.

Now we live by faith in the Son of God who loves us and gave His life for us. In this session, we will begin to examine the transition from who we once were, into who we are now.

In 1 Corinthians 6:9, God's Word tells us that the unrighteous will not inherit the kingdom of God. Then, in 1 Corinthians 6:11, the Word tells us that is not who we are. We have been washed, justified, and sanctified in the name of Jesus Christ and by the Spirit of our God!

One of the strategies of the enemy is to accuse believers of being unrighteous (Revelation 12:10). The enemy knows your weaknesses and he accuses you specifically in the areas where you are wounded and believing lies. Sadly, many people have been so well trained to accuse themselves, that they don't need any assistance from the enemy.

The key point is that you are no longer unrighteous. You are redeemed. You have been washed, justified, and sanctified by the blood of Jesus Christ. Something actually changed when you put your faith in Jesus Christ.

For the word of the cross is folly to those who are perishing, but to us who are being saved it is the power of God. – 1 Corinthians 1:18

The word of the cross is the power of God to us who are being saved (1 Corinthians 1:18).

Let's look at some of the Scriptures that describe what the power of God has done through the cross.

Read Ephesians 1:3-14

Ephesians 1:7

What do we now have through Jesus' blood?

_____

_____

Read Colossians 1:11-14

Colossians 1:14

What have we been given, through Jesus, now that the Father has transferred us from darkness into the kingdom of His beloved Son?

_____

_____

Read Galatians 3:10-14

Galatians 3:13

What has Christ done for us regarding the curse of the law?

_____

_____

Read Hebrews 9:11-22

Hebrews 9:12

What has Jesus done for us by means of His own blood?

_____

_____

Hebrews 9:15

What has Jesus mediated for us through His death?

_____

_____

Read Titus 2:11–14

Titus 2:14

What has Jesus done for us by giving Himself for us?

_____

_____

In Titus 3:4-5, the Word tells us that the goodness and loving kindness of God saves us not by our own works done in righteousness, but according to His mercy by the washing of regeneration and renewal of the Holy Spirit.

This is the transforming power of the cross. We have been forgiven and redeemed through the blood of Christ by the washing of regeneration and renewal of the Holy Spirit. The cross frees us from the law. We no longer work for righteousness; it is given freely by God's mercy.

Let's look at the definitions of "forgiveness" and "redemption" and then examine the Scripture in light of these definitions.

Forgiveness – the Greek word used here is **aphesis** (Strong's G859)
It means: release, as from bondage or imprisonment – forgiveness or pardon of sins (as if they have never been committed) – remission of penalty

Redemption – the Greek word used here is **apolytrōsis** (Strong's G629)
It means: a releasing effected by a payment of ransom – liberation procured by the payment of a ransom – redemption – deliverance

An expression of the Scripture including the fullness of those definitions could be:

Through the blood of Christ, by the power of the Holy Spirit, we have been released from any curse, penalty, bondage, transgression, trespass, or imprisonment. Jesus paid the ransom for our sins with His own blood, thus securing for us an eternal redemption, releasing us as if the sins were never committed.

Consider this...

What are the truths that God is revealing to you personally about these Scriptures?

How could believing these truths affect your life?

_____

_____

_____

What are some practical steps you can take to experience these truths in your life?

_____

_____

_____

Now ask the Holy Spirit to empower you and make these truths more real in your life.

Statement of Faith

I have redemption in Jesus through His blood. My sins have been forgiven according to the riches of His grace. God lavished all this upon me, in all wisdom and insight, making known to me the mystery of His will, according to His purpose, which He set forth in Christ. Christ redeemed me from the curse of the law by becoming a curse for me. In Christ Jesus, the blessing of Abraham came to me, so that I could receive the promised Spirit through faith. Jesus is the mediator of a new covenant for me. He called me and gave me the promised eternal inheritance. Jesus gave Himself for me to redeem me from all lawlessness and to purify me for Himself.

When the goodness and loving kindness of God our Savior appeared, He saved us, not because of works done by us in righteousness, but according to His own mercy, by the washing of regeneration and renewal of the Holy Spirit, whom He poured out on us richly through Jesus Christ our Savior, so that being justified by His grace we might become heirs according to the hope of eternal life. – Titus 3:4-7

ARE YOU JUSTIFIED?

As we learned in the beginning of this session, 1 Corinthians 6:11 tells us that we are washed, justified, and sanctified in the name of Jesus Christ.

Read Romans 3:21-31

Romans 3:24

We are justified _____

_____

Romans 3:26

In Christ Jesus, God demonstrates His righteousness and is the justifier of _____

_____

Romans 3:28

One is justified _____

_____

Read Romans 5:1-11

Romans 5:1

We have been justified _____

we have _____

_____

Romans 5:9

We have now been justified _____

how much more then _____

_____

Read Titus 3:1-8

Titus 3:7

Being justified _____

we become _____

Let's look at the definition of "justified" and then examine the Scripture in light of this definition.

> **Justified** – The Greek word used is **dikaioō** (Strong's G1344)
> It means: to render righteous or as such ought to be – to declare or pronounce one to be just, righteous, or as such ought to be

An expression of the Scripture including the fullness of this definition could be:

You have freely been rendered and declared righteous and just, by His grace, as the Lord says you ought to be.

Consider this...

What are the truths that God is revealing to you personally about these Scriptures?

_____

_____

_____

How could believing these truths affect your life?

_____

_____

_____

What are some practical steps you can take to experience these truths in your life?

_____

_____

_____

Now ask the Holy Spirit to empower you and make these truths more real in your life.

Statement of Faith

God demonstrates His righteousness by being my justifier. I have been justified freely by God's grace, through the redemption that is in Christ Jesus. Therefore, since I am justified by faith, I have peace with God through our Lord Jesus Christ. I am an heir according to the hope of eternal life by the blood of Jesus.

I have been crucified with Christ. It is no longer I who live, but Christ who lives in me. And the life I now live in the flesh I live by faith in the Son of God, who loved me and gave Himself for me. – Galatians 2:20

ARE YOU SANCTIFIED?

Read John 17:16-19

John 17:17

We are sanctified by_____

John 17:19

Jesus sanctified Himself, so that_____

_____

Read 1 Thessalonians 5:23-24

1 Thessalonians 5:23

Now may the God of peace Himself_____

_____

_____

Read Hebrews 10:5-18

Hebrews 10:10

We are sanctified through _____

_____

Hebrews 10:14

For by a single offering_____

_____

Let's look at the definition of "sanctified" and then examine the Scripture in light of this definition.

> **Sanctified** – The Greek word used here is **hagiazō** (Strong's G37)
> It means: to render or to be venerable or holy – to be separate and dedicated to God – to purify – to be dedicated or consecrated to God – to purify internally by renewing of the soul

An expression of the Scripture including the fullness of that definition could be:

> *You have been declared holy and purified, and have been dedicated to God through the sacrifice of Christ Jesus.*

Consider this...

What are the truths that God is revealing to you personally about these Scriptures?

_____

_____

_____

How could believing these truths affect your life?

_____

_____

_____

What are some practical steps you can take to experience these truths in your life?

_____

_____

_____

Now ask the Holy Spirit to empower you and make these truths more real in your life.

Statement of Faith

I have been sanctified by the word Jesus spoke over me; the word is truth. God Himself, the God of peace, sanctifies me completely. He has perfected me for all time, through the single offering of Jesus Christ.

> For through the law I died to the law, so that I might live to God.
> – Galatians 2:19

As believers, one of the paradigms that we live in is the paradigm of the sanctification process. We have been sanctified and perfected for all time by the single offering of Jesus Christ, and we are in the process of sanctification. We will examine this paradigm further at the end of Session Three.

ARE YOU RECONCILED?

Read Ephesians 2 and then review the chart below:

WE WERE		WE ARE
Dead in our trespasses	▶ ▶ ▶	Alive together with Christ
Dead in our sins	▶ ▶ ▶	Saved by grace
Following the course of this world	▶ ▶ ▶	A holy temple in the Lord
Sons of disobedience	▶ ▶ ▶	Created in Christ for good works
Children of wrath	▶ ▶ ▶	Members of God's household
Gentiles in the flesh	▶ ▶ ▶	Saints
Separate from Christ	▶ ▶ ▶	His workmanship created in Christ
Alienated from the commonwealth	▶ ▶ ▶	Fellow citizens
Strangers to the covenant of promise	▶ ▶ ▶	Seated in heavenly realms
Hopeless	▶ ▶ ▶	Raised up with Him
Without God	▶ ▶ ▶	A dwelling place for God
Far off	▶ ▶ ▶	Brought near
Hostile	▶ ▶ ▶	Reconciled as one in peace

If you have put your faith in Jesus Christ, you are no longer who you once were.

Read John 15:1-5

John 15:3

You are already _____

_____

Read Romans 5:6-11

Romans 5:10

When we were enemies, we were _____

_____

How much more, now that we are reconciled_____

_____

Romans 5:11

We rejoice in God, through our Lord Jesus Christ through whom_____

_____

Read Romans 6:5-19

Romans 6:11

You also must consider yourself_____

and_____

Romans 6:18

You have been_____

you have become_____

Read 2 Corinthians 5:16-19

2 Corinthians 5:17

In Christ, you are_____

The old_____

the new_____

2 Corinthians 5:18

All this is from God, who_____

_____

Read Galatians 5:1-6

Galatians 5:1

For freedom, Christ has _____

_____

Read Colossians 1:15-23

Colossians 1:21-22

You, who once were _____

_____

He has now _____

_____

_____

Let's look at the definition of "reconciled" and then examine the Scripture in light of this definition.

> **Reconciled** – the Greek word used here is **apokatallassō** (Strong's G604)
> It means: to change – to reconcile completely – exchange – return to favor – to be reconciled to one – to reestablish proper relationship – to receive one into favor – to make things right with one another

An expression of the Scripture including the fullness of that definition could be:

For freedom, Christ has set you free. You are a new creation. The old has passed and the new has come. All this is from God, who has received you into favor, restored you, and brought you into proper and right relationship with Him. He has reconciled you completely.

Consider this...

What are the truths that God is revealing to you personally about these Scriptures?

_____

_____

_____

How could believing these truths affect your life?

_____

_____

_____

What are some practical steps you can take to experience these truths in your life?

_____

_____

_____

Now ask the Holy Spirit to empower you and make these truths more real in your life.

Statement of Faith

I am saved by grace and made alive together with Christ. God has raised me up with Christ and seated me with Him in heavenly places. Through the blood of Jesus Christ, He brought me near to Himself. I have been set free from sin and have become a slave to righteousness. For freedom, Christ has set me free. I am clean because of the word Jesus spoke over me. He reconciled me through His body, and now presents me holy, blameless, and free from accusation. I am a new creation in Christ. The old is gone and the new has come. All this is from God, who reconciled me to Himself, and made me a member of His household. God created me in Christ Jesus for good works. I am dead to sin and alive to God.

> From now on, therefore, we regard no one according to the flesh. Even though we once regarded Christ according to the flesh, we regard Him thus no longer. – 2 Corinthians 5:16

15

THE RESTORATION PROCESS

The life we live now, we live by faith. A simple definition of faith is:

Believing and living the truth of God's Word through the power of the Holy Spirit.

With that understanding of faith, let's process through the following Scripture and see what the Lord reveals to you.

In Him we have redemption through His blood, the forgiveness of our trespasses, according to the riches of His grace. – Ephesians 1:7

Take a moment to pray and invite God to meet with you in this process. Reflect on Ephesians 1:7, and ask the Holy Spirit to reveal the truth of what God is saying in that Scripture.

List the truth that was revealed to you:

_____

_____

_____

_____

_____

Review Ephesians 1:7 one more time and ask the Lord to reveal any of your thoughts or feelings that may be opposed to that Scripture.

Ask the Lord what lies you believe that are connected to those thoughts and feelings.

List the lies that were revealed:

_____

_____

_____

_____

Remember to draw near to God and stay aware that He is present with you. As you review this list, ask the Lord if there is anyone you need to forgive that may have taught you these lies or hurt you with these lies. Remember, forgiveness is not about accusation or understanding why someone did what they did; it is about releasing through the blood of Jesus.

As the Lord leads, express the forgiveness out loud.

Remember to forgive and release through the blood of Jesus by the power of the Holy Spirit.

"In Jesus' name, I choose to forgive_____for 'teaching me' or 'hurting me' with the lie that_____."

Now that you have forgiven, you can deal with the lies themselves. Since God revealed to you that these are lies, you can repent from believing the lies by breaking agreement and renouncing them out loud.

"In Jesus' name, I break agreement and renounce the lie that_____."

Take a moment and let the Holy Spirit comfort you and restore you.

Ask the Lord:

"Lord, is there anything You want to give me in return for all the lies I have released to You?"

As you receive them, you can list them here:

_____

_____

_____

Jesus has forgiven all your trespasses and sins. Forgiving yourself is merely coming into agreement with Him.

Forgive yourself out loud:

"Jesus, I come into agreement with You, and I completely forgive myself for any way I believed those lies. I release all the lies, and I forgive myself."

Rest here for a moment and enjoy the freedom!

This is where it gets fun. Review the Scripture again.

In Him we have redemption through His blood, the forgiveness of our trespasses, according to the riches of His grace – Ephesians 1:7

Ask the Lord:

"Now that I have renounced the lies and forgiven everyone, what are the promises and truths available to me in that Scripture?"

List what He reveals to you:

When the LORD restored the fortunes of Zion, we were like those who dream. Then our mouth was filled with laughter, and our tongue with shouts of joy; then they said among the nations, "The LORD has done great things for them." The LORD has done great things for us; we are glad. – Psalm 126:1-3

Let yourself dream and think about these truths and promises. Let the Holy Spirit reveal how they would affect your life if you believed them and lived them. What would your life look like—be like? How could it affect your relationships, attitude, career, family, etc.?

List the effects below:

What are some practical steps you can take to experience this in your life?

Let yourself receive from the Holy Spirit and ask Him to empower you, make these truths and promises more real in your life, and help you fulfill the dreams He has given you.

Thank the Lord out loud:

"Thank You, Lord, for the truth that_____and thank You for the promise(s) of _____. I receive them from You by faith and ask that You empower them through the Holy Spirit in my life."

Before moving on, write down any additional thoughts now that you have had time to pray, dream, and receive from the Lord.

_____

_____

_____

_____

_____

You are completely released, redeemed, and forgiven through the blood of Christ, by the washing of regeneration and renewal of the Holy Spirit, according to the riches of His grace. Praise God!

IDENTITY

These are some of the ways the Lord describes you, as we learned from this session. This is who the Lord declares that you are:

Saved

Redeemed

Forgiven

Redeemed from the curse

Eternally secure

Called

Purified

His people

His possession

Saved by Him

Crucified with Christ

Loved

Sanctified in truth

Sanctified completely

Blameless

Dead to sin

Perfected for all time

Alive to God

A fellow citizen

Raised up with Him

A dwelling place for God

Brought near

Reconciled as one in peace

Clean because of Jesus' Word

Reconciled to God

Reconciled

Alive to God in Jesus

Zealous for good works

Washed

Regenerated

Renewed

Justified by His grace

Justified by faith

Justified apart from works

Justified by His blood

Alive together with Christ

A holy temple in the Lord

His workmanship

A saint

Created in Christ Jesus for good works

A member of God's household

Sanctified through the offering of Jesus Christ

In Christ

A new creation

New

A minister of reconciliation

Set free

Free

Holy

An heir according to the hope of eternal life

Above reproach before Him

Created in Christ

Review this list of identity descriptions and write down those that stand out and inspire you:

Take a moment to pray and reflect on these descriptions. Write down a statement of faith of your own:

_____

_____

_____

_____

_____

_____

Declare this over yourself out loud.

Wrap Up

Ask God:

"What is the main thing You want me to learn from this session?"

_____

_____

"How can this affect my life now?"

_____

_____

"What are some practical steps I can take to experience this in my life?"

_____

_____

_____

Take a few moments right now and thank God for what He revealed to you.

Practical Take Away Tips

Read through the identity descriptions, memorize them, and declare them over yourself.

Re-read and declare the statements of faith from this session, both the given statements and the one you created for yourself.

Remind yourself of the truths and promises that God revealed to you. Continue to dream and ask God to make them more real in your life.

Copy and use the blank Restoration Process on page 165 of the Appendix with the following Scriptures, or any Scriptures that God highlights to you.

- Romans 5:1

- 1 Thessalonians 5:23-24

- 2 Corinthians 5:17

Session 2
Am I Alive?

CONTENTS

ARE YOU A SINNER?

In Session One, we looked at the amazing transition from who we were into who we are now. We looked at the redemption and reconciliation that Jesus provided for us. In this session, we will examine the reality of our new identity and how that identity is alive in the Spirit, not dead in sin.

> But God, being rich in mercy, because of the great love with which He loved us, even when we were dead in our trespasses, made us alive together with Christ—by grace you have been saved—and raised us up with Him and seated us with Him in the heavenly places in Christ Jesus, so that in the coming ages He might show the immeasurable riches of His grace in kindness toward us in Christ Jesus. For by grace you have been saved through faith. And this is not your own doing; it is the gift of God, not a result of works, so that no one may boast. For we are His workmanship, created in Christ Jesus for good works, which God prepared beforehand, that we should walk in them.
> – Ephesians 2:4-10

God, in His rich mercy and love for us, made us alive together with Christ when we were dead in our sins and trespasses.

Let's start with an analogy. Before a couple is married, they are each a single, individual person. Once they are married, they enter into a covenant together and become one flesh (Ephesians 5:31). They are no longer the single individual person; they are together, united, and one.

With that in mind, imagine if the bride in a marriage continually believed and referred to herself as a single person even though she is married to her husband. She does this regardless of how many times the husband reminds her and tells her that he loves her, that he gave everything to be with her, that they are married, and that she is now one flesh with him. What if, every time she had a conversation with her husband, she would start out the conversation with, "Thank you for marrying me. I know I am just a single person and there is nothing good in me, but…"?

Think about that for a moment and answer these questions:

How do you think believing that lie would affect the intimacy in that relationship?

How do you think that may affect the bride's confidence in the relationship?

How do you think that may affect the bride's behavior?

Now here is the rest of the analogy:

> **For I feel a divine jealousy for you, since I betrothed you to one husband, to present you as a pure virgin to Christ. – 2 Corinthians 11:2**

As His church, we are the bride of Christ. In the same way the people in our analogy were single before they were married, we were sinners that were once dead in our sin (Ephesians 2:1). When we put our faith in Jesus, He renewed us through the washing and renewal of the Holy Spirit, and we are now a new, righteous creation that is one with God.

With that in mind, imagine if we, as the bride of Christ, continually believed and referred to ourselves as "just a sinner" even though we are a new creation in Christ (2 Corinthians 5:17). Imagine if we remained stuck in this mindset regardless of how many times God reminded us that He loves us and that He gave His only Son to be a sin sacrifice for us. What if, every time we had a conversation with God, we would start out with, "Thank you for saving me. I know I am just a sinner and there is nothing good in me, but…"?

Think about that for a moment and answer these questions:

How do you think believing that lie would affect the intimacy in relationship with God?

How do you think that may affect the confidence of a follower of Jesus?

How do you think that may affect the behavior of a follower of Jesus?

_____

_____

Sadly, many well-meaning followers of Jesus believe and declare that they are still "just a sinner." They think they are honoring God and being humble before Him. This lie is one of the most debilitating and destructive lies influencing the body of Christ. It robs believers of their true identity, confidence, intimacy with God, and purpose.

> **For Christ also suffered once for sins, the righteous for the unrighteous, that He might bring us to God, being put to death in the flesh but made alive in the Spirit. – 1 Peter 3:18**

Jesus died on the cross for us while we were still unrighteous sinners. He suffered and was sacrificed, so that we may be reconciled unto God the Father. Jesus condemned sin in us and put it to death. We are now the righteousness of God. We are alive in the Spirit. Now that is good news!

> **I am speaking in human terms, because of your natural limitations. For just as you once presented your members as slaves to impurity and to lawlessness leading to more lawlessness, so now present your members as slaves to righteousness leading to sanctification. – Romans 6:19**

Presenting yourself as a sinner leads to more sin. Presenting yourself as righteous leads to holiness and sanctification.

ARE YOU DEAD TO SIN?

Let's delve into the differences between "dead in sin" and "alive in the Spirit." Allow God to reveal to you in His Scriptures the importance of what you think about yourself.

Romans 3:12

All have turned aside; together_____

_____

Romans 3:23

We have all sinned, and_____

_____

Romans 5:12

Just as sin came into the world through one man_____

and so death spread to_____because_____

Ephesians 2:1

And you were_____

Colossians 2:13a

You who were_____

_____

All have sinned and fallen short of the glory of God. Together, we had all turned away from God and become worthless. We were dead in our sins and in the uncircumcision of our flesh.

In Romans 7:5, depending on the translation, the Word tells us that we were in the "flesh" or "sinful nature." The following is an example of three different translations:

For while we were living in the 'flesh', our sinful passions, aroused by the law, were at work in our members to bear fruit for death. – ESV

For when we were controlled by the 'sinful nature', the sinful passions aroused by the law were at work in our bodies, so that we bore fruit for death. – NIV

For when we were in the 'flesh', the sinful passions which were aroused by the law were at work in our members to bear fruit to death. – NKJ

Let's look at the definition of "flesh/sinful nature" and then examine the Scripture in light of this definition.

> **Flesh/sinful nature** – the Greek word used here is **sarx** (Strong's G4561)
> It means: flesh – the body – human nature – a living creature – the earthly nature of man apart from divine influence

An expression of the Scripture including the fullness of that definition could be:

We all used to live in the sinful passions aroused by the law. We were dead in our sins and we lived according to the human, earthly nature apart from God and apart from divine influence.

Now let's examine what God did with us while we were still just sinners:

Galatians 2:20a

I have been_____

Colossians 2:20a

With Christ you have_____

_____

Colossians 3:3

You have_____

Romans 8:3

God sent His own Son in the likeness of sinful flesh and for sin_____

_____

Read Romans 6:1-11

Romans 6:2

By no means!_____ how can we live in it any longer?

Romans 6:3

All of us have been baptized_____

We were baptized into_____

Romans 6:4a

We were buried_____

Romans 6:5a

We have been_____

Romans 6:6

We know that_____

in order that_____

so that we would_____

Romans 6:7

For one who has died_____

Romans 6:8a

Now if we have_____

Romans 6:10a

For the death He died_____

Romans 6:11a

You also must consider yourself_____

In Romans 6:6, the Word tells us that we were crucified with Him so that the body of sin might be brought to nothing.

Let's look at the definition of "nothing" and then examine the Scripture in light of this definition.

Nothing – the Greek word used here is **katargeō** (Strong's G2673)
It means: to render inactive – to put out of use – to destroy – to make completely inoperative – to cause to cease – to do away with – to be severed from

An expression of the Scripture including the fullness of that definition could be:

You know that your old self was crucified with Christ in order that your body of sin might be rendered inactive, destroyed, made completely inoperative, and done away with, so that you could be completely severed from it, no longer enslaved to sin.

Consider this...

What are the truths that God is revealing to you personally about these Scriptures?

_____

_____

_____

How could believing these truths affect your life?

_____

_____

_____

What are some practical steps you can take to experience these truths in your life?

_____

_____

_____

Now ask the Holy Spirit to empower you and make these truths more real in your life.

Statement of Faith

My old self has been crucified with Christ. When I was still just a sinner, Jesus condemned sin in my flesh so that my old body of sin was brought to nothing. I was united with Him in His death and buried with Him in baptism. I am dead to sin, no longer a slave to sin, and I have been set free from sin in Christ Jesus.

The thief comes only to steal and kill and destroy. I came that they may have life and have it abundantly. I am the good shepherd. The good shepherd lays down His life for the sheep. – John 10:10-11

We were dead in our sins and trespasses. Jesus became flesh and then condemned sin in the flesh. On the cross, our old sinful self was brought to nothing and crucified with Him. Through the sacrifice of Jesus on the cross there is nothing left of that old self.

ARE YOU ALIVE IN THE SPIRIT?

Read Romans 5:15-21

Romans 5:15

The free gift_____

_____

the free gift is by_____

Romans 5:17

Those who receive the grace and the free gift of righteousness_____

_____

Romans 5:18

Jesus' one act of righteousness_____

_____

Romans 5:19

Through Jesus' obedience_____

Romans 5:20

Where sin increased,_____

Romans 5:21

As sin reigned in death_____

leading to_____

Read Romans 6:1-11

Romans 6:4

Just as Christ was raised from the dead by our Father_____

_____

Romans 6:5

If we have been united with Him in death_____

_____

Romans 6:8

If we have died with Christ, we believe_____

Romans 6:10

The life He lives_____

Romans 6:11

Consider yourselves dead to sin and_____

Read Romans 6:20-23

Romans 6:22

Now that you have been set free_____

the benefit you reap is_____

Romans 6:23

The free gift of God is_____

Read Romans 8:9-11

Romans 8:11

If the Spirit dwells in you, He who raised Jesus will also _____

_____

Read 2 Corinthians 5:16-21

2 Corinthians 5:17

If anyone is in Christ _____

The old has passed away _____

Read Galatians 2:17-21

Galatians 2:19

I died to the law so that _____

Galatians 2:20

It is no longer I who live, but _____

The life I live now, I live by _____

_____

Read Ephesians 2:1-7

Ephesians 2:5

Even when we were dead in our trespasses, God made us _____

_____

Read Colossians 2:8-15

Colossians 2:13

You, who were dead, God made _____

_____

Read 1 Peter 3:18

1 Peter 3:18

Being put to death in the flesh, we have been made _____

In Ephesians 2:5, the Word says that by grace we have been saved.

Let's look at the definition of "saved" and then examine the Scripture in light of this definition.

> **Saved** – the Greek word used here is **sozo** (Strong's G4982)
> It means: to save – heal – restore to health – deliver – make whole

An expression of the Scripture including the fullness of that definition could be:

By grace through faith you are forgiven, redeemed, reconciled, washed clean, justified, sanctified, set free, righteous, saved, healed, delivered, made whole, alive, and united with Jesus in life to live for God.

Consider this...

What are the truths that God is revealing to you personally about these Scriptures?

_____

_____

_____

How could believing these truths affect your life?

_____

_____

_____

What are some practical steps you can take to experience these truths in your life?

_____

_____

_____

Now ask the Holy Spirit to empower you and make these truths more real in your life.

Statement of Faith

By grace, I am united with Christ in His resurrection. It is no longer my old self who lives, but Christ who lives in me. By faith, I am made righteous through Jesus, and I reign with Him in the newness of life. The old has passed away and the new has come. I am saved by grace, and grace reigns through me for eternal life. I am a new creation in Christ. I am alive in the Spirit and I live to God.

But God, being rich in mercy, because of the great love with which He loved us, even when we were dead in our trespasses, made us alive together with Christ—by grace you have been saved—and raised us up with Him and seated us with Him in the heavenly places in Christ Jesus. – Ephesians 2:4-6

IS YOUR MIND SET ON THE SPIRIT?

Romans 6:11

Consider yourselves dead to sin and_____

Read Romans 8:1-11

Romans 8:1

There is therefore now_____

Romans 8:2

For the law of the Spirit of life has_____

_____

Romans 8:5

For those who live according to the flesh_____

_____

but those who live according to the Spirit_____

_____

Romans 8:6

For to set the mind on the flesh _____

but to set the mind on the Spirit _____

Romans 8:7

For the mind that is set on the flesh _____

_____

Romans 8:8

Those who are in the flesh _____

Romans 8:9

You, however, are not in the flesh _____

if in fact _____

Anyone who does not have the Spirit of Christ _____

Romans 8:10

But if Christ is in you, although the body is dead because of sin _____

_____

Romans 8:11

If the Spirit dwells in you, He who raised Christ Jesus from the dead _____

_____

through His Spirit _____

Read Ephesians 5:15-21

Ephesians 5:18

Do not get drunk with wine, but be _____

Read Colossians 3:1-4

Colossians 3:2

Set your minds _____

not on things _____

Colossians 3:3

For you have died _____

In Romans 6:11, the Word tells us that we also must consider ourselves dead to sin and alive to God in Christ Jesus.

Let's look at the definition of "consider" and then examine the Scripture in light of this definition.

> **Consider** – the Greek word used here is **logizomai** (Strong's G3049)
> It means: to reckon – count – compute – calculate – count over –to take into account – consider – deem – judge – determine –purpose – decide

An expression of the Scripture including the fullness of that definition could be:

You are not in the flesh; you are in the Spirit. Decide and purpose to count and judge yourself dead to sin and alive to God. You are pleasing to God, and the Spirit dwells in you. Let yourself be filled with the Spirit and live according to the Spirit. Set your mind on the things of the Spirit.

Consider this...

What are the truths that God is revealing to you personally about these Scriptures?

....

....

....

How could believing these truths affect your life?

....

....

....

What are some practical steps you can take to experience these truths in your life?

_____

_____

_____

Now ask the Holy Spirit to empower you and make these truths more real in your life.

Statement of Faith

I am set free in Christ, and my life is hidden with Him in God. I am not in the flesh, I am not controlled by the flesh, and I do not live according to the flesh. I am in the Spirit and live according to the Spirit. The Spirit dwells in me and gives me life. I am alive to God and I belong to Christ Jesus. He lives in me, and I have life and peace because my mind is set on the things of the Spirit.

> So you also must consider yourselves dead to sin and alive to God in Christ Jesus. – Romans 6:11

That is a statement of humility! Humility accepts that there are no behaviors, deeds, works, actions, or offerings that we can give to be righteous. Only the righteous offering of Jesus Christ is what makes us righteous. True humility is laying down all the worldly principles, requirements, laws, expectations, and standards that we have established to manage righteousness. True humility is accepting the truth of who God says we are.

What we think, what we believe, and what we declare matters.

> Such is the confidence that we have through Christ toward God. Not that we are sufficient in ourselves to claim anything as coming from us, but our sufficiency is from God. – 2 Corinthians 3:4-5

ARE YOU RENEWED?

Romans 6:13

Present yourselves to God as _____

_____

and present your members _____

_____

Ephesians 4:23

Be renewed _____

Ephesians 4:24

Put on the new self _____

_____

Colossians 3:10

Put on the new self _____

_____

2 Timothy 2:15

Do your best and be diligent to present yourself _____

_____

God is telling us to no longer have a mind set on the sinful nature. That old nature has been cut off from us and is no longer who we are. He tells us to put on the new self that is righteous, approved, holy, alive, and has no need to be ashamed. He is telling us to be renewed in the spirit of our mind and come into agreement with who He declares us to be. Being alive in the Spirit, we have our minds set on the things of the Spirit, and we can present ourselves to Him as who He created us to be.

Read Romans 12:1-2

Romans 12:1

I appeal to you therefore, brothers _____

to present your bodies _____

which is your _____

I appeal to you therefore, brothers, by the mercies of God, to present your bodies as a living sacrifice, holy and acceptable to God, which is your spiritual worship. – Romans 12:1

Let's look at the definitions of "mercies," "spiritual," and "worship," and then examine the Scripture in light of these definitions.

Mercies – the Greek word used here is **oiktirmos** (Strong's G3628)
It means: compassion – the heart of compassion – where compassion resides – mercy – emotions – longings – pity

Spiritual – the Greek word used here is **logikos** (Strong's G3050)
It means: pertaining to speech – reason – logic – spiritual – agreeable – reasonable – logical

Worship – the Greek word used here is **latreia** (Strong's G2999)
It means: service – service to God – worship – performing sacred services

An expression of the Scripture including the fullness of those definitions could be:

I appeal to you therefore, brothers, by the deep longing, compassion, and mercies of God, to present your bodies as a living sacrifice, holy and acceptable to God, which is your reasonable, logical, and spiritual act of service and worship to Him.

Romans 12:2

Do not be conformed_____

but be transformed_____

Do not be conformed to this world, but be transformed by the renewal of your mind, that by testing you may discern what is the will of God, what is good and acceptable and perfect. – Romans 12:2

Let's look at the definition of "discern" and then examine the Scripture in light of this definition.

> **Discern** – the Greek word used here is **dokimazō** (Strong's G1381)
> It means: test – examine – prove – recognize as genuine – discern – approve – deem worthy

An expression of the Scripture including the fullness of that definition could be:

Do not be conformed to this world, but be transformed by the renewal of your mind, that you may recognize the genuine will of God, and then approve and prove what is good and acceptable and perfect.

Let's refer back to the analogy that we started with in the very beginning of this session. Now that you are forgiven, redeemed, washed clean, justified, sanctified, reconciled, righteous, and alive, what do you think about the appropriateness of presenting yourself to God as just a sinner with nothing good in you?

_____

_____

_____

Consider this...

What are the truths that God is revealing to you personally about these Scriptures?

_____

_____

_____

How could believing these truths affect your life?

_____

_____

_____

What are some practical steps you can take to experience these truths in your life?

_____

_____

_____

Now ask the Holy Spirit to empower you and make these truths more real in your life.

Statement of Faith

I have been brought from death to life. All of me is new. I have been created after the likeness of God as an instrument of true righteousness and holiness. I am an approved, holy, and acceptable living sacrifice, being renewed in the knowledge of my Creator. I can discern the will of God – what is His good, acceptable, and perfect will.

The time is fulfilled, and the kingdom of God is at hand; repent and believe in the gospel. – Mark 1:15

THE RESTORATION PROCESS

The life we live now, we live by faith. A simple definition of faith is:

Believing and living the truth of God's Word, through the power of the Holy Spirit.

With that understanding of faith, let's process through the following Scripture and see what the Lord reveals to you.

I have been crucified with Christ. It is no longer I who live, but Christ who lives in me. And the life I now live in the flesh I live by faith in the Son of God, who loved me and gave Himself for me. – Galatians 2:20

Take a moment to pray and invite God to meet with you in this process. Reflect on Galatians 2:20, and ask the Holy Spirit to reveal the truth of what God is saying in that Scripture.

List the truth that was revealed to you:

_____

_____

_____

_____

Review Galatians 2:20 one more time and ask the Lord to reveal any of your thoughts or feelings that may be opposed to that Scripture.

Ask the Lord what lies you believe that are connected to those thoughts and feelings.

List the lies that were revealed:

_____

_____

_____

_____

Remember to draw near to God and stay aware that He is present with you. As you review this list, ask the Lord if there is anyone you need to forgive that may have taught you these lies or hurt you with these lies. Remember, forgiveness is not about accusation or understanding why someone did what they did; it is about releasing through the blood of Jesus.

As the Lord leads, express the forgiveness out loud.

Remember to forgive and release through the blood of Jesus by the power of the Holy Spirit.

"In Jesus' name, I choose to forgive_____for 'teaching me' or 'hurting me' with the lie that_____."

Now that you have forgiven, you can deal with the lies themselves. Since God revealed to you that these are lies, you can repent from believing the lies by breaking agreement and renouncing them out loud.

"In Jesus' name, I break agreement and renounce the lie that_____."

Take a moment and let the Holy Spirit comfort you and restore you.

Ask the Lord:

"Lord, is there anything You want to give me in return for all the lies I have released to You?"

As you receive them, you can list them here:

Jesus has forgiven all your trespasses and sins. Forgiving yourself is merely coming into agreement with Him.

Forgive yourself out loud:

"Jesus, I come into agreement with You and I completely forgive myself for any way I believed those lies. I release all the lies, and I forgive myself."

Rest here for a moment and enjoy the freedom!

This is where it gets fun. Review the Scripture again.

> I have been crucified with Christ. It is no longer I who live, but Christ who lives in me. And the life I now live in the flesh I live by faith in the Son of God, who loved me and gave Himself for me. – Galatians 2:20

Ask the Lord:

"Now that I have renounced the lies and forgiven everyone, what are the promises and truths available to me in that Scripture?"

List what He reveals to you:

When the LORD restored the fortunes of Zion, we were like those who dream. Then our mouth was filled with laughter, and our tongue with shouts of joy; then they said among the nations, "The LORD has done great things for them." The LORD has done great things for us; we are glad. – Psalm 126:1-3

Let yourself dream and think about these truths and promises. Let the Holy Spirit reveal how they would affect your life if you believed them and lived them. What would your life look like—be like? How could it affect your relationships, attitude, career, family, etc.?

List the effects below:

_____

_____

_____

_____

What are some practical steps you can take to experience this in your life?

_____

_____

_____

Let yourself receive from the Holy Spirit and ask Him to empower you, make these truths and promises more real in your life, and help you fulfill the dreams He has given you.

Thank the Lord out loud:

"Thank You, Lord, for the truth that_____and thank You for the promise(s) of _____. I receive them from You by faith and ask that You empower them through the Holy Spirit in my life."

Before moving on, write down any additional thoughts now that you have had time to pray, dream, and receive from the Lord.

_____

_____

_____

_____

_____

Review

What words do you remember from Session One that describe who God says you are?

_____

_____

_____

_____

IDENTITY

These are some of the ways the Lord describes you, as we learned from this session. This is who the Lord declares that you are:

Greatly loved

Alive together with Christ

Saved

Raised up with Him

Seated in heavenly places

In Christ Jesus

Saved through faith

His workmanship

Created in Christ Jesus for good works

Betrothed

A pure virgin to Christ

Brought to God

Justified

Alive with Christ

A slave of God

Alive through His Spirit that dwells in me

A new creation

New

Dead to the law

Forgiven

Dead in the flesh

Alive in the Spirit

Free from the law of sin and death

Set free in Christ Jesus

Not in the flesh but in the Spirit

A slave to righteousness

Crucified with Christ

Loved

Dead to the spirits of the world

Hidden with Christ in God

Dead to sin

Baptized into Christ Jesus

United with Him in resurrection

Crucified with Him

Set free from sin

Alive to God in Christ

Righteous

Reigning in life

Filled with the Spirit

Brought from death to life

An instrument for righteousness

Renewed

Created after the likeness of God

Created in true righteousness

Created in true holiness

An approved worker

Unashamed

A living sacrifice

Holy

Acceptable to God

Renewed in knowledge after the image of my Creator

Review this list of identity descriptions and write down the ones that stand out and inspire you:

_____

_____

_____

_____

Take a moment to pray and reflect on these descriptions and write down a statement of faith of your own:

_____

_____

_____

_____

Declare this over yourself out loud.

Wrap Up

Ask God:

"What is the main thing You want me to learn from this session?"

_____

_____

"How can this affect my life now?"

_____

_____

"What are some practical steps I can take to experience this in my life?"

_____

_____

_____

Take a few moments right now and thank God for what He revealed to you.

Practical Take Away Tips

Read through the identity descriptions, memorize them, and declare them over yourself.

Re-read and declare the statements of faith from this session, both the given statements and the one you created for yourself.

Remind yourself of the truths and promises that God revealed to you. Continue to dream and ask God to make them more real in your life.

Copy and use the blank Restoration Process on page 165 of the Appendix with the following Scriptures, or any Scriptures that God highlights to you.

- Romans 5:17

- Romans 6:4

- Romans 6:22-23

- 2 Corinthians 5:17

Session 3
Am I Righteous?

CONTENTS

ARE YOU RIGHTEOUS?

Believing that we are righteous is key to our life in Christ. What we believe will directly affect our lives. It will affect how we live and what we do. The righteous shall live by faith (Romans 1:17).

Are you righteous? Many followers of Jesus struggle with this question.

In Session One, we looked at the amazing transition from who we were into who we are now. Because of God's grace and mercy, through our faith in the blood sacrifice of Jesus, we are forgiven, redeemed, washed clean, justified, sanctified, and reconciled. In Session Two, we looked at the reality of our new identity, and how that identity is alive in the Spirit and not dead in sin. None of that is by works or by the law. All of it is by the regeneration and renewal of the Holy Spirit. In this session, we will look at our new, righteous identity.

> But that is not the way you learned Christ!—assuming that you have heard about Him and were taught in Him, as the truth is in Jesus, to put off your old self, which belongs to your former manner of life and is corrupt through deceitful desires, and to be renewed in the spirit of your minds, and to put on the new self, created after the likeness of God in true righteousness and holiness. – Ephesians 4:20-24

As the truth is in Jesus, put off your old self, be renewed in the spirit of your mind, and put on your new self, created in true righteousness and holiness.

Read Romans 3:21-26

Romans 3:21a

Now_____

_____

Romans 3:22

the_____

through_____

to and for all_____

there is_____

Read Romans 6:15-19

Romans 6:17

Thanks be to God, that though you were once slaves of sin_____

_____

_____

Romans 6:18

Having been set free, have become_____

Read 1 Corinthians 1:26-31

1 Corinthians 1:30

Because of Him_____

who became to us_____

_____

Read 2 Corinthians 5:16-21

2 Corinthians 5:21

For our sake He made Him_____

so that in Him we might become_____

Read Romans 4:1-25

Romans 4:3

What does the Scripture say?_____

and it was_____

Romans 4:5

The one who does not work but_____

_____

his faith_____

Romans 4:7

Blessed are those_____

_____

Romans 4:8

Blessed is the man_____

Romans 4:13

The promise to Abraham did not come through_____

but through_____

Romans 4:16

Therefore, that is why_____

in order that_____

and be guaranteed and sure_____

not only to those of the law_____

who is_____

Romans 4:22

Therefore, that is why his faith was_____

Romans 4:23

The words were not written_____

Romans 4:24

but also_____

It will be imputed, credited, and counted_____

_____

Let's look at the definition of "righteousness" and then examine the Scripture in light of this definition.

> **Righteousness** – The Greek word used is **dikaiosynē** (Strong's G1343)
> It means: the state of who you are as you ought to be – righteousness – the condition acceptable to God – approved of God – integrity – virtue – purity of life – rightness – correctness

An expression of the Scripture including the fullness of that definition could be:

Now that you have put your faith in Jesus, you are as you ought to be. You are right with God, acceptable, approved, virtuous, and pure in life, apart from the law. You are blessed, and your sins will never be counted against you.

Consider this...

What are the truths that God is revealing to you personally about these Scriptures?

_____

_____

_____

How could believing these truths affect your life?

_____

_____

_____

What are some practical steps you can take to experience these truths in your life?

_____

_____

_____

Now ask the Holy Spirit to empower you and make these truths more real in your life.

Statement of Faith

By faith, as an offspring of Abraham, I am guaranteed to be an heir of the promise. I am in Christ. God is my wisdom, righteousness, sanctification, and redemption. I have become the righteousness of God in Jesus Christ. I am blessed. My sins are forgiven, covered, and will never be counted against me.

I appeal to you therefore, brothers, by the mercies of God, to present your bodies as a living sacrifice, holy and acceptable to God, which is your spiritual worship. Do not be conformed to this world, but be transformed by the renewal of your mind, that by testing you may discern what is the will of God, what is good and acceptable and perfect. – Romans 12:1-2

Coming into agreement with God about who you are, and presenting yourself to Him as a living sacrifice, holy and acceptable to Him, is your spiritual act of worship. Do not be conformed to this world, but be transformed by the renewing of your mind. With your renewed mind, you will be able to discern the will of God and know that you are righteous by faith in Jesus, apart from the law.

ARE YOU RIGHTEOUS, PRACTICALLY?

The gospel is the power of God for salvation to everyone who believes (Romans 1:16). Now that you have believed unto salvation, you are in Christ. He has become your wisdom, righteousness, sanctification, and redemption. In Him, you have been transformed into the righteousness of God.

Many followers of Jesus believe that even though God sees them as righteous (positional righteousness), they are required to pursue righteous behavior to be fully righteous (practical righteousness).

In this section, we will look at the concept of positional and practical righteousness in the Scriptures. Let's start out by reviewing what God says about how we are righteous, and how He imputed, credited, and counted that righteousness to us. The chart on the next page shows the different Scriptures that address this.

THE RIGHTEOUSNESS OF GOD

Romans 1:17 ▶ ▶ ▶ from faith

Romans 3:21 ▶ ▶ ▶ apart from the law

Romans 3:22 ▶ ▶ ▶ through faith

Romans 3:22 ▶ ▶ ▶ believe

Romans 4:3 ▶ ▶ ▶ believe God

Romans 4:5 ▶ ▶ ▶ not by works

Romans 4:5 ▶ ▶ ▶ trust God

Romans 4:5 ▶ ▶ ▶ your faith

Romans 4:6 ▶ ▶ ▶ apart from works

Romans 4:9 ▶ ▶ ▶ faith

Romans 4:11 ▶ ▶ ▶ by faith

Romans 4:13 ▶ ▶ ▶ of faith

Romans 4:22 ▶ ▶ ▶ your faith

Romans 4:24 ▶ ▶ ▶ believe in Him

Romans 9:30 ▶ ▶ ▶ by faith

Romans 10:6 ▶ ▶ ▶ based on faith

Galatians 3:6 ▶ ▶ ▶ believe God

Philippians 3:9 ▶ ▶ ▶ not of my own

Philippians 3:9 ▶ ▶ ▶ not of the law

Philippians 3:9 ▶ ▶ ▶ through faith

Philippians 3:9 ▶ ▶ ▶ from God

Philippians 3:9 ▶ ▶ ▶ depends on faith

Hebrews 11:7 ▶ ▶ ▶ comes by faith

James 2:23 ▶ ▶ ▶ believe God

As you read that list, you may have noticed that there is something missing in regard to practical righteousness. None of the Scriptures that express the righteousness of God mention anything about our behavior.

There are some Scriptures that have been used to promote the concept of behavioral or practical righteousness, so let's look at those.

Who is wise and understanding among you? By his good conduct let him show his works in the meekness of wisdom. – James 3:13

We will look at our conduct more specifically in Session Four, but for now, let's look at James 3:13 in context.

Read James 3

James 3:5

The tongue is a small member and_____

James 3:6

The tongue is_____

The tongue is set among our members, staining the whole body, setting on fire the entire

course of life, and set on fire by_____

James 3:8

No human can tame the tongue._____

_____

James 3:10

From out of the same mouth_____

My brothers, these things_____

James 3:14

But if you have_____

Do not boast and_____

James 3:15

This is not wisdom that comes from above, it is_____

_____

James 3:16

For where envy, jealousy, and selfish ambition exist_____

_____

James 3:17

But the wisdom from above is_____

_____

_____

James 3:18

And now_____

_____

Let's look at the definitions of "conduct" and "show" and then examine the Scripture in light of these definitions.

> **Conduct** – The Greek word used is **anastrophē** (Strong's G390)
> It means: manner of life – conduct – behavior
>
> **Show** – The Greek word used is **deiknyō** (Strong's G1166)
> It means: to show – expose to the eyes – to give evidence or proof of a thing – to show by words or teach

An expression of the Scripture including the fullness of those definitions could be:

> *You, as one with the wisdom from above, let that wisdom—that pure, good, fruitful, peaceable, gentle, impartial, open to reason, and merciful wisdom—show and prove itself by your conduct.*

If you remember from the definition of righteousness earlier in this session, we are as we ought to be. We are right with God, apart from the law and regardless of our works. We are acceptable, approved, and pure in life. Manifesting evil from our tongue is not who we are and how things ought to be.

James 3:13, in context, seems to be focusing on what is in our hearts. What is in our hearts will manifest. It seems to be encouraging us to let the wisdom that is pure and peaceful manifest from our hearts into a harvest of good works, because that is who we are.

Looking at this verse in context, knowing that the righteous will live by faith, and that we are righteous by faith in Jesus, what do you think God is expressing in James 3:13?

_____

_____

_____

Let's look at another Scripture.

> But as He who called you is holy, you also be holy in all your conduct, since it is written, "You shall be holy, for I am holy." – 1 Peter 1:15-16

Before moving forward, let's review. In Session One, we looked at the truth that we have been sanctified by the blood offering of Jesus. Remember, sanctified is hagiazō, which means to be made holy. We have been made holy by the blood offering of Jesus.

Let's look at the definitions of "holy" and "be" and then examine the Scripture in light of these definitions.

Holy – The Greek word used is **hagios** (Strong's G40)
It means: holy – saint

Be – The Greek word used is **ginomai** (Strong's G1096)
It means: to become – to come into existence – begin to be – receive being – to arise – to be made – finished

An expression of the Scripture including the fullness of that definition could be:

In the same way that He who called you is holy, receive holiness. Become a holy saint in all manner of your life and conduct. It is written, you will be made holy because He is holy.

Now let's look at 1 Peter 1:15-16 in context:

> Therefore, preparing your minds for action, and being sober-minded, set your hope fully on the grace that will be brought to you at the revelation of Jesus Christ. As obedient children, do not be conformed to the passions of your former ignorance, but as He who called you is holy, you also be holy in all your conduct, since it is written, "You shall be holy, for I am holy." And if you call on Him as Father who judges impartially according to each one's deeds, conduct yourselves with fear throughout the time of your exile, knowing that you were ransomed from the futile ways inherited from your forefathers, not with perishable things such as silver or gold, but with the precious blood of Christ, like that of a lamb without blemish or spot. He was foreknown before the foundation of the world but was made manifest in the last times for the sake of you who through Him are believers in God, who raised Him from the dead and gave Him glory, so that your faith and hope are in God. Having purified your souls by your obedience to the truth for a sincere brotherly love, love one another earnestly from a pure heart, since you have been born again, not of perishable seed but of imperishable, through the living and abiding word of God. – 1 Peter 1:13-23

Looking at 1 Peter 1:15-16 in context, knowing that the righteous will live by faith, that we are righteous by faith in Jesus, and that we have been made holy by the blood offering of Jesus:

What do you think God is expressing in 1 Peter 1:15-16?

_____

_____

_____

Let's look at one more Scripture.

> Stand therefore, having fastened on the belt of truth, and having put on the breastplate of righteousness – Ephesians 6:14

As we have seen in the Scriptures concerning the righteousness of God, behavior is not listed as a way to become righteous. The Lord has shown us, in His Word, that we will manifest what we believe in our heart. In the "Are You Renewed?" section of Session Two, we looked at the concept of "putting on" the new self. We learned that this is done through the attitude and spirit of our mind, not by behavior (Ephesians 4:23-24). The same word for "putting on" is used in both Ephesians 4:24 and Ephesians 6:14.

Let's look at the definition of "putting on" and then examine the Scripture in light of this definition.

> **Putting on** – the Greek word used here is **endyō** (Strong's G1746)
> It means: to draw on – to sink into (clothing) – put on – to dress – to clothe oneself

An expression of the Scripture including the fullness of that definition could be:

Stand therefore, having fastened on the belt of truth. Put on the breastplate of righteousness, in the attitude and spirit of your mind.

Remembering that the righteous will live by faith, that we are righteous by faith in Jesus, that our behavior cannot make us righteous, and that we have been made holy by the blood offering of Jesus:

What do you think God is expressing in Ephesians 6:14?

_____

_____

_____

In Session Two, we looked at the falsehood of still being a sinner. The lie that we are still just sinners, and the pursuit of behavioral righteousness, are looped together. If we are deceived into thinking that we are still just sinners, and then tricked by the enemy into pursuing behavioral righteousness, we will enter into a cycle of sin and condemnation.

As you believe the lie that you are still just a sinner, and then try to behave righteously, you will manifest that lie from your heart and confirm it every time you fail to perform to the false expectations you have placed on yourself. This will inevitably lead to more sinful behavior (Romans 6:19). These false expectations and this false humility may have the appearance of wisdom, but lack any value at stopping the indulgence of sin.

But seek first the kingdom of God and His righteousness, and all these things will be added to you. – Matthew 6:33

ARE YOU PURSUING RIGHTEOUSNESS?

Throughout the Scriptures, the Lord tells us who we are (the indicative), and then He tells us what it looks like to be who we are (the imperative). Jesus Himself demonstrated this for us. He believed the truth of His identity, and that is what He manifested. As we believe the indicative, it will manifest from our hearts into the imperative, in all aspects of our lives. In this section, we will look at what it means to pursue the righteousness of God by faith.

Matthew 6:33

What are we to seek first?

_____

Proverbs 21:21

If we pursue righteousness, what will we find?

_____

We have learned that the righteousness of God is of God, through God, and by God. We have received His righteousness as a gift through faith in Jesus Christ.

Seeking and pursuing righteousness is simply a pursuit of the truth of who God is and who we are in Him. God says that we are righteous by faith in Christ. Our behavior never made us righteous, and it will never affect our righteousness. Pursuing righteous behavior is not a pursuit of the righteousness of God, and it will not manifest righteousness. Pursuing the truth that we are righteous by faith will manifest life, righteousness, and honor.

God wants us to seek first the kingdom and His righteousness. Seeking His righteousness has nothing to do with our behavior, works, deeds, or the law—it is of faith, by faith, and through faith in Jesus. So let's look at what the Scripture says about faith.

Hebrews 11:1

What is faith?

_____

_____

Hebrews 11:6

Without faith_____for whoever would

draw near to God must believe that He exists and rewards those who seek Him.

Review the previous Scriptures concerning righteousness and faith. What does it look like to pursue righteousness?

_____

_____

By faith, you are a new creation. You are renewed in the knowledge of your righteousness in God through the power of the Holy Spirit. You are pleasing to God by believing that you are righteous even before you see the evidence of your righteousness in your behavior.

Before moving on, take a moment to reflect upon this. Feel free to write down any thoughts that you may have.

_____

_____

_____

_____

What About Sin?

It would be foolish to say that now that we are righteous, we never sin. However, as a follower of Jesus, it would be just as foolish to say that because we sin, we are not righteous.

Let's review:

By faith in Jesus Christ, all of our sins have been forgiven, as if they had never happened. Our sins and lawless acts are remembered no more. We have been sanctified completely, and have been justified by grace as a gift. We have been declared holy, pure, righteous, and just. We are reconciled with God. We have been set free, washed clean, and are now a new creation. We are no longer dead in our sin; we are alive in Christ.

This is righteousness. We are right with God. Believing this truth is pleasing to God.

Now the question is:

If this is the truth, why do we still sin?

The answer is simple:

We don't fully believe that we are the righteousness of God.

Let's look at James 2:17, 26:

James 2:17

Faith by itself_____

James 2:26

Faith apart from works_____

The Scripture tells us that faith by itself, if there are no deeds to go along with that faith, is dead. What we believe, we will live. The righteous will live by faith. What we believe will manifest itself in our lives. The sinful behaviors in our lives are the fruit of the lies we believe. If there are no good works to match what we say we believe, maybe that belief is dead. Pursuing a behavior that looks righteous is not the righteousness of God. God wants us to pursue His righteousness by faith. Faith in His righteousness will allow us to manifest the pure and peaceable wisdom from above. This will result in a harvest of good works and a manner of life that ought to be, because that is who we are.

> Do not be conformed to this world, but be transformed by the renewal of your mind, that by testing you may discern what is the will of God, what is good and acceptable and perfect. – Romans 12:2

> And to be renewed in the spirit of your minds, and to put on the new self, created after the likeness of God in true righteousness and holiness. – Ephesians 4:23-24

It is time to be renewed in the spirit of our mind, to be transformed by the renewing of our mind, and to no longer be conformed to the pattern of this world. It is time to put off the old self that pursues a behavioral righteousness, and put on the new self that seeks first the righteousness of God. Pursuing the righteousness of God, by faith, will manifest the good works of that righteousness.

Do you believe that you are righteous?

> The Spirit of the Lord God is upon Me, because the Lord has anointed Me to bring good news to the poor; He has sent Me to bind up the brokenhearted, to proclaim liberty to the captives, and the opening of the prison to those who are bound; to proclaim the year of the Lord's favor, and the day of vengeance of our God; to comfort all who mourn; to grant to those who mourn in Zion— to give them a beautiful headdress instead of ashes, the oil of gladness instead of mourning, the garment of praise instead of a faint spirit; that they may be called oaks of righteousness, the planting of the Lord, that He may be glorified. – Isaiah 61:1-3

The following is a list of some of the truths that God states about your righteousness in Him. Take a moment and boldly read through these out loud, agreeing with Him about who you are.

- *I am righteous by faith.*

- *I am the righteousness of God.*

- *I am righteous apart from the law.*

- *I am righteous by faith in Jesus.*

- *I am righteous by believing God.*

- *I am righteous by trusting God.*

- *I am righteous not by work.*

- *I am righteous apart from works.*

- *I am righteous by believing in Him.*

- *I am righteous based on faith.*

- *I am righteous not on my own.*

- *I am righteous not of the law.*

- *I am righteous through faith.*

- *My righteousness comes by faith, not by works.*

Thank You, Jesus, that You became sin, and condemned sin in me, so that I have become the righteousness of God, by faith in You.

IS THE LAW FULFILLED IN YOU?

Read Romans 8:1-17

Romans 8:2

What has the law of the Spirit of life done for us?

Romans 8:3

What did God do that the law could not do?

Romans 8:4

Why did God send His Son to condemn sin in the flesh?

Romans 8:5

What do those that live according to the Spirit do?

Romans 8:6

Setting our mind on the Spirit is?

In Romans 8:4, the Word tells us that God sent His own Son in order that the righteous requirements of the law might be fulfilled in us.

Let's look at the definition of "fulfilled" and then examine the Scripture in light of this definition.

> **Fulfilled** – The Greek word used is **plēroō** (Strong's G4137)
> It means: to make full – to fill up – to fill to the full – to cause to abound – to furnish or supply liberally – to render full – to complete – to make complete in every particular – to make perfect – to accomplish – to carry into effect – to bring into realization

An expression of the Scripture including the fullness of that definition could be:

God sent His Son, in the likeness of sinful flesh, to condemn sin in the flesh. He did this in order that the righteous requirements of the law could be made perfect and complete in you. You are filled, to the full, with these righteous requirements, and He will accomplish them. He will bring them into realization in your life, while you walk according to the Spirit.

Consider this...

What are the truths that God is revealing to you personally about these Scriptures?

_____

_____

_____

How could believing these truths affect your life?

_____

_____

_____

What are some practical steps you can take to experience these truths in your life?

_____

_____

_____

Now ask the Holy Spirit to empower you and make these truths more real in your life.

Statement of Faith

I am in Christ and set free from condemnation. God sent His own Son, in the likeness of sinful flesh, to condemn sin in my flesh. The righteous requirements of the law are fulfilled in me. I walk according to the Spirit, with my mind set on the things of the Spirit. I am in the Spirit, and my mind is filled with life and peace. The Spirit dwells in me, and my spirit is alive because of righteousness.

> For if, because of one man's trespass, death reigned through that one man, much more will those who receive the abundance of grace and the free gift of righteousness reign in life through the one man Jesus Christ. – Romans 5:17

What is The Process of Sanctification?

Let's review what we have learned so far. In Session One, we looked at the truth that we are redeemed, justified, sanctified, reconciled and perfected for all time by the single offering of Jesus Christ. In Session Two, we looked at the truth that, by grace, we are no longer sinners. We are dead to sin, and alive in the Spirit. In this session, we looked at the truth that we are the righteousness of God by faith, that we are holy because He is holy, and that Jesus condemned sin in our flesh and fulfilled the righteous requirements of the law in us.

So if this is true, what is the process of sanctification? The process of sanctification is not a process of becoming holy and righteous. The Word tells us that we are holy and righteous in Christ. Either we are holy and righteous in Christ, or we are not in Christ. The Lord tells us to be transformed by the renewing of our mind. He tells us to put off the old self, be renewed in the spirit of our mind, and put on the new self. The transformation is in our mind, by faith. The process of sanctification is a process of believing the truth of our holy and righteous identity in Christ. As we have learned, what we believe in our heart, we will manifest in our behavior. As we believe the truth of our holy and righteous identity, our lives will be transformed and we will manifest that truth.

THE RESTORATION PROCESS

The life we live now, we live by faith. A simple definition of faith is:

Believing and living the truth of God's Word, through the power of the Holy Spirit.

With that understanding of faith, let's process through the following Scriptures and see what the Lord reveals to you.

And because of Him you are in Christ Jesus, who became to us wisdom from God, righteousness and sanctification and redemption.
– 1 Corinthians 1:30

For our sake He made Him to be sin who knew no sin, so that in Him we might become the righteousness of God. – 2 Corinthians 5:21

Take a moment to pray and invite God to meet with you in this process. Reflect on 1 Corinthians 1:30 and 2 Corinthians 5:21, and ask the Holy Spirit to reveal the truth of what God is saying in those Scriptures.

List the truth that was revealed to you:

_____

_____

_____

_____

_____

Review 1 Corinthians 1:30 and 2 Corinthians 5:21 one more time and ask the Lord to reveal any of your thoughts or feelings that may be opposed to those Scriptures.

Ask the Lord what lies you are believing that are connected to those thoughts and feelings.

List the lies that were revealed:

_____

_____

_____

_____

Remember to draw near to God and stay aware that He is present with you. As you review this list, ask the Lord if there is anyone you need to forgive that may have taught you these lies or hurt you with these lies. Remember, forgiveness is not about accusation or understanding why someone did what they did; it is about releasing through the blood of Jesus.

As the Lord leads, express the forgiveness out loud.

Remember to forgive and release through the blood of Jesus by the power of the Holy Spirit.

"In Jesus' name, I choose to forgive_____ for 'teaching me' or 'hurting me' with the lie that_____."

Now that you have forgiven, you can deal with the lies themselves. Since God revealed to you that these are lies, you can repent from believing the lies by breaking agreement and renouncing them out loud.

"In Jesus' name, I break agreement and renounce the lie that_____."

Take a moment and let the Holy Spirit comfort you and restore you.

Ask the Lord:

"Lord, is there anything You want to give me in return for all the lies I have released to You?"

As you receive them, you can list them here:

_____

_____

_____

Jesus has forgiven all your trespasses and sins. Forgiving yourself is merely coming into agreement with Him.

Forgive yourself out loud:

"Jesus, I come into agreement with You and I completely forgive myself for any way I believed those lies. I release all the lies, and I forgive myself."

Rest here for a moment and enjoy the freedom!

This is where it gets fun. Review the Scriptures again.

> And because of Him you are in Christ Jesus, who became to us wisdom from God, righteousness and sanctification and redemption.
> – 1 Corinthians 1:30

> For our sake He made Him to be sin who knew no sin, so that in Him we might become the righteousness of God. – 2 Corinthians 5:21

Ask the Lord:

"Now that I have renounced the lies and forgiven everyone, what are the promises and truths available to me in those Scriptures?"

List what He reveals to you:

_____

_____

_____

_____

_____

> When the LORD restored the fortunes of Zion, we were like those who dream. Then our mouth was filled with laughter, and our tongue with shouts of joy; then they said among the nations, "The LORD has done great things for them." The LORD has done great things for us; we are glad. – Psalm 126:1-3

Let yourself dream and think about these truths and promises. Let the Holy Spirit reveal how they would affect your life if you believed them and lived them. What would your life look like—be like? How could it affect your relationships, attitude, career, family, etc.?

List the effects below:

_____

_____

_____

_____

What are some practical steps you can take to experience this in your life?

_____

_____

_____

Let yourself receive from the Holy Spirit and ask Him to empower you, make these truths and promises more real in your life, and help you fulfill the dreams He has given you.

Thank the Lord out loud:

"Thank You, Lord, for the truth that_____and thank You for the promise(s) of _____. I receive them from You by faith and ask that You empower them through the Holy Spirit in my life."

Before moving on, write down any additional thoughts now that you have had time to pray, dream, and receive from the Lord.

_____

_____

_____

_____

Review

What words do you remember from Session One and Session Two that describe who God says you are?

_____

_____

_____

_____

IDENTITY

These are some of the ways the Lord describes you, as we learned from this session. This is who the Lord declares that you are:

Created after the likeness of God

Created in true righteousness

Created in true holiness

Set free in Christ Jesus

Reigning in life

The righteousness of God

Justified

Obedient from the heart

Set free from sin

A slave of righteousness

In Christ Jesus

Righteous

Blessed

Forgiven

Covered

Abraham's offspring

The righteousness of faith

A brother/sister

A living sacrifice

Holy

Acceptable to God

A peacemaker

An obedient child

A believer

Purified

Born again of imperishable seed

An oak of righteousness

Review this list of identity descriptions and write down the ones that stand out and inspire you:

_____

_____

_____

_____

Take a moment to pray and reflect on these descriptions and write down a statement of faith of your own:

_____

_____

_____

_____

_____

_____

Declare this truth over yourself out loud.

Remember, God says you are righteous.

Wrap Up

Ask God:

"What is the main thing You want me to learn from this session?"

_____

_____

"How can this affect my life now?"

_____

_____

"What are some practical steps I can take to experience this in my life?"

_____

_____

_____

Take a few moments right now and thank God for what He revealed to you.

Practical Take Away Tips

Read through the identity descriptions, memorize them, and declare them over yourself.

Re-read and declare the statements of faith from this session, both the given statements and the one you created for yourself.

Remind yourself of the truths and promises that God revealed to you. Continue to dream and ask God to make them more real in your life.

Copy and use the blank Restoration Process on page 165 of the Appendix with the following Scriptures, or any Scriptures that God highlights to you.

- Romans 8:2-4

- Ephesians 4:23-24

Session 4

Am I Fruitful?

CONTENTS

79

ARE YOU FRUITFUL?

From the very beginning of time, we were created to be fruitful, to express the truth of who we are, and to have dominion over what the Lord has given us. We were created to steward, learn, grow, and produce. There is a divine intentionality, purpose, and plan for each and every one of us.

There is beauty in His creation; there is beauty in you. God created you in His own image. In the image of Himself, He created you.

Then God said, "Let Us make man in Our image, after Our likeness. And let them have dominion over the fish of the sea and over the birds of the heavens and over the livestock and over all the earth and over every creeping thing that creeps on the earth."

So God created man in His own image, in the image of God He created him; male and female He created them.

And God blessed them. And God said to them, "Be fruitful and multiply and fill the earth and subdue it, and have dominion over the fish of the sea and over the birds of the heavens and over every living thing that moves on the earth." And God said, "Behold, I have given you every plant yielding seed that is on the face of all the earth, and every tree with seed in its fruit. You shall have them for food. And to every beast of the earth and to every bird of the heavens and to everything that creeps on the earth, everything that has the breath of life, I have given every green plant for food." And it was so. And God saw everything that He had made, and behold, it was very good. And there was evening and there was morning, the sixth day. – Genesis 1:26-31

In this session, we will examine the fruit of our faith.

Read Psalm 139:13-16

Psalm 139:13

For You formed and created_____

_____in my mother's womb.

Psalm 139:14

I praise You, for_____

_____are Your works

my soul_____

Read Ephesians 2:1-10

Ephesians 2:10

For we are_____

_____in Christ Jesus_____

which God prepared_____

that we should_____

God created you, in His image, to walk in the good works that He prepared for you beforehand.

Read Philippians 1:3-11

Philippians 1:4-5

I thank my God in remembrance of you, always in every prayer…with joy,

because_____

Philippians 1:6

And I am sure of this, that He who began_____

will_____

Philippians 1:7a

I hold you in my heart, in the defense and confirmation of the gospel because you all

_____

Philippians 1:11

filled with_____

which comes_____

_____

In Philippians 1:6, the Word tells us that the Lord will bring to completion the good work He began in us.

Let's look at the definition of "completion" and then examine the Scripture in light of this definition.

> **Completion** – the Greek word used here is **epiteleō** (Strong's G2005)
> It means: to bring to an end – accomplish – complete

An expression of the Scripture including the fullness of that definition could be:

You are God's workmanship. You were created, in Christ, for good works which He prepared beforehand. He is sure that the works He began in you will be accomplished and completed by Him.

Consider this...

What are the truths that God is revealing to you personally about these Scriptures?

_____

_____

_____

How could believing these truths affect your life?

_____

_____

_____

What are some practical steps you can take to experience these truths in your life?

_____

_____

_____

Now ask the Holy Spirit to empower you and make these truths more real in your life.

Statement of Faith

I am fearfully and wonderfully made in God's image. Before I was even born, God prepared good works for me to walk in. He will bring these to completion. I am a partner with Him in the gospel of grace. I am filled with the fruit of righteousness through Jesus.

> To this end we always pray for you, that our God may make you worthy of His calling and may fulfill every resolve for good and every work of faith by His power, so that the name of our Lord Jesus may be glorified in you, and you in Him, according to the grace of our God and the Lord Jesus Christ. – 2 Thessalonians 1:11-12

In Session Three, we looked at the difference between the righteousness of God and the facade of behavioral righteousness. As we learned from the Scripture, managing our behavior is not the pursuit of righteousness. We also learned that our behavior is the fruit of what we actually believe about God and ourselves.

Does Our Behavior Matter?

Read Romans 13:8-14

Romans 13:12

the day is at hand. So then let us_____

_____

Read Ephesians 4:17-25

Ephesians 4:17

I testify in the Lord that you must_____

_____

in the_____

Ephesians 4:22

_____which belongs to

your former manner of life and is corrupt through deceitful desires

Read Colossians 3:1-17

Colossians 3:2

Set your minds on things that are above,_____

Colossians 3:5

Put to death therefore_____

Colossians 3:8

But now you must_____

_____

Colossians 3:9

Do not lie to one another, seeing that_____

_____

Read Romans 6:1-4

Romans 6:1-2

Are we to continue in sin that grace may abound?_____

How can we who died to sin still live in it?

Let's review. In Session One through Session Three, we looked at the truth that even while we were sinners, Christ forgave us for all of our sin and redeemed us. We are no longer sinners; we are the righteousness of God in Christ. We are no longer dead in sin; we are alive in Christ. In Session Two, we looked specifically at being renewed in the spirit of our minds - "putting off" the old dead self, and "putting on" the new living self.

For to set the mind on the flesh is death, but to set the mind on the Spirit is life and peace. For the mind that is set on the flesh is hostile to God, for it does not submit to God's law; indeed, it cannot. Those who are in the flesh cannot please God. You, however, are not in the flesh but in the Spirit, if in fact the Spirit of God dwells in you. Anyone who does not have the Spirit of Christ does not belong to Him. But if Christ is in you, although the body is dead because of sin, the Spirit is life because of righteousness. – Romans 8:6-10

If you believe that you are still just a sinner, and you try to manage your sin, you have your mind set on the flesh. This will produce sin and death. Believing the truth that you are the righteousness of God is setting your mind on the Spirit. This will produce life and peace.

If you want to stop sinning and start walking in newness of life, stop trying to manage your behavior in your own effort. Repent from the lies that are causing you to manifest those sinful behaviors, and start believing the truth of who God says you are. Be transformed by the renewing of your mind. Put off the old self, and put on the new self. Come into agreement with Him, in the spirit and attitude of your mind, and be who He created you to be. With this partnership in faith, He will manifest His presence in you and fulfill the works He created you to walk in.

Woe to you, scribes and Pharisees, hypocrites! For you clean the outside of the cup and the plate, but inside they are full of greed and self-indulgence. You blind Pharisee! First clean the inside of the cup and the plate, that the outside also may be clean. – Matthew 23:25-26

The mind set on sin is death; the mind set on the Spirit is life and peace. What you believe in your heart is what you will manifest in your behavior. Instead of the meaningless task of managing behavior (cleaning the outside of the cup), you could set your mind on the Spirit, and change the way you think about yourself. Cleaning the inside will take care of the outside.

God created you in His own image. He created you to walk in the works He prepared for you. These works are perfectly suited to who you are. He fulfills these works in you through His power and will. Partnering in faith with Him will allow Him to fulfill these works in you and through you.

ARE YOU EQUIPPED?

Read 2 Corinthians 9:6-9

2 Corinthians 9:8

And God is able to make_____

so that having all sufficiency_____

you may abound_____

Read Colossians 1:9-14

Colossians 1:9

you may be filled with_____

in all_____

Colossians 1:10

so as to walk in a manner_____

fully_____

bearing fruit_____

and increasing_____

Colossians 1:11

May you be strengthened_____

according to_____

_____

Colossians 1:12

giving thanks to the Father, who has_____

to share in_____

Read Hebrews 13:20-21

Hebrews 13:20-21

Now may the God of peace, through the blood of the everlasting covenant, make_____

you complete, and equip you_____

_____

working in us_____

through Jesus Christ, to whom_____

Who Fulfills Your Good Works?

Read Philippians 2:12-13

Philippians 2:13

for it is_____

both to_____

for His_____

Read 1 Thessalonians 2:9-13

1 Thessalonians 2:13

when you received the word of God you heard from us_____

_____

_____

which is_____

Read 2 Thessalonians 1:11-12

2 Thessalonians 1:11

we pray that our God may_____

and that He may_____

and every act or work_____

2 Thessalonians 1:12

so that the name of our Lord Jesus_____

according to_____

Read 2 Thessalonians 2:16-17

2 Thessalonians 2:16

May Jesus Christ, and God our Father,_____

and gave us_____

_____

2 Thessalonians 2:17

comfort your hearts and_____

_____

Let's look at the definition of "work" and then examine the Scripture in light of this definition.

> **Work** – the Greek word used here is **ergon** (Strong's G2041)
> It means: business – employment – that which one undertakes to do – undertaking – any product whatever – an act – any thing accomplished by hand – deed – thing done

An expression of the Scripture including the fullness of that definition could be:

God makes all grace abound to you. You are fully pleasing to Him, and have all sufficiency, in all things, at all times. You bear fruit and abound in every good work, business, undertaking, accomplishment, and deed that you do. It is God who works in you to will, work, accomplish, and produce for His good pleasure.

Consider this...

What are the truths that God is revealing to you personally about these Scriptures?

_____

_____

_____

How could believing these truths affect your life?

_____

_____

_____

What are some practical steps you can take to experience these truths in your life?

_____

_____

_____

Now ask the Holy Spirit to empower you and make these truths more real in your life.

Statement of Faith

All grace abounds to me. I have all sufficiency, in all things, at all times, to abound in every good work. I am filled with the knowledge of His will, with all spiritual wisdom and understanding, so that I can walk in a manner worthy of the Lord. I am fully pleasing to Him, bearing fruit in every good work. I am strengthened with all power according to His glorious might. He made me worthy of His calling, and I am qualified and equipped with everything good. God is fulfilling His will in me. He is doing the work He prepared for me, for His good pleasure. Jesus is glorified in me, and I am glorified in Jesus. God loves me and eternally comforts me with hope through grace.

Follow the pattern of the sound words that you have heard from me, in the faith and love that are in Christ Jesus. By the Holy Spirit who dwells within us, guard the good deposit entrusted to you.
– 2 Timothy 1:13-14

Those who have received the abundance of grace, and the free gift of righteousness, reign in life through Jesus. We died with Christ and were raised to life with Him, so that we could walk in newness of life. The life we live now, we live by faith in Jesus, who loves us and gave Himself for us. We walk by faith and live by faith.

ARE YOU LIVING IN FAITH?

Read Philippians 1:19-27

Philippians 1:21

For me, to live is_____

Philippians 1:22

If I am to live, that means_____

Read 1 Thessalonians 1:2-3

1 Thessalonians 1:3

remembering before our God and Father your_____

and_____

and_____

Read Galatians 5:6

The only thing that counts is_____

Read Galatians 5:16-26

Galatians 5:16

But I say, walk by the Spirit,_____

Galatians 5:18

But if you are led by the Spirit,_____

Galatians 5:22-23

But the fruit of the Spirit is_____

_____

against such things_____

Galatians 5:24

And those who belong to Christ Jesus_____

with its_____

Galatians 5:25

If we live by the Spirit,_____

_____

Read Ephesians 5:8-9

Ephesians 5:8

for at one time you were darkness,_____

_____

Ephesians 5:9

for the fruit of that is_____

> You, however, have followed my teaching, my conduct, my aim in life,
> my faith, my patience, my love, my steadfastness – 2 Timothy 3:10

Read Titus 2:11-14

Titus 2:11

For the grace of God_____

_____

Titus 2:12

training and teaching us to_____

_____

Titus 2:14

Jesus gave Himself for us to _____

and to _____

who are _____

Read Titus 3:4-8

Titus 3:6

Holy Spirit has been _____

_____

Titus 3:7

being justified by His grace we _____

_____

Titus 3:8

those who believe in God may _____

_____

These things are _____

Read John 6:28-29

John 6:29

This is the work of God, _____

_____

Let's look at the definition of "believe" and then examine the Scripture in light of this definition.

> **Believe** – the Greek word used here is **pisteuō** (Strong's G4100)
> It means: to think to be true – to be persuaded – to credit – to place confidence in – to trust – faith

An expression of the Scripture including the fullness of that definition could be:

Your work is to trust, be confident in, and have faith in Jesus. Believe that He has crucified your old sinful flesh. Be convinced that your life is a life in Christ, led by the Spirit. Believe that as you walk by the Spirit, as a child of light, the fruit of that light is good, right, and true. Be confident in the grace that is training you to renounce all ungodliness. Trust God that this is true. Walk in the Spirit, and you will not gratify the desires of your old dead flesh.

Consider this...

What are the truths that God is revealing to you personally about these Scriptures?

_____

_____

_____

How could believing these truths affect your life?

_____

_____

_____

What are some practical steps you can take to experience these truths in your life?

_____

_____

_____

Now ask the Holy Spirit to empower you and make these truths more real in your life.

Statement of Faith

My flesh, with its passions and desires, has been crucified. I live in Christ. My life in Christ is a life of fruitful labor. My fruitful labor is faith working through love. I walk in the Spirit and I am led by the Spirit. I am filled with the fruit of righteousness. I am a child of light: a good, right, and true light in the Lord. I live by the Spirit and keep in step with the Spirit. The grace of God is training me to renounce all ungodliness, and live an upright, godly life. Jesus purified me as His own and made me zealous for good works. Holy Spirit has been richly poured out on me through Jesus, and I am devoted to good works.

> For it is God who works in you, both to will and to work for His good pleasure. – Philippians 2:13

> Only let us hold true to what we have attained. – Philippians 3:16

THE RESTORATION PROCESS

The life we live now, we live by faith. A simple definition of faith is:

Believing and living the truth of God's Word, through the power of the Holy Spirit.

With that understanding of faith, let's process through the following Scriptures and see what the Lord reveals to you.

> Be renewed in the spirit of your minds, and put on the new self, created after the likeness of God in true righteousness and holiness. – Ephesians 4:23-24

> And I am sure of this, that He who began a good work in you will bring it to completion at the day of Jesus Christ. – Philippians 1:6

Take a moment to pray and invite God to meet with you in this process. Reflect on Ephesians 4:23-24 and Philippians 1:6, and ask the Holy Spirit to reveal the truth of what God is saying in those Scriptures.

List the truth that was revealed to you:

_____

_____

_____

_____

_____

Review Ephesians 4:23-24 and Philippians 1:6 one more time and ask the Lord to reveal any of your thoughts or feelings that may be opposed to those Scriptures.

Ask the Lord what lies you are believing that are connected to those thoughts and feelings.

List the lies that were revealed:

_____

_____

_____

_____

Remember to draw near to God and stay aware that He is present with you. As you review this list, ask the Lord if there is anyone you need to forgive that may have taught you these lies or hurt you with these lies. Remember, forgiveness is not about accusation or understanding why someone did what they did; it is about releasing through the blood of Jesus.

As the Lord leads, express the forgiveness out loud.

Remember to forgive and release through the blood of Jesus by the power of the Holy Spirit.

"In Jesus' name, I choose to forgive_____for 'teaching me' or 'hurting me' with the lie that_____."

Now that you have forgiven, you can deal with the lies themselves. Since God revealed to you that these are lies, you can repent from believing the lies by breaking agreement and renouncing them out loud.

"In Jesus' name, I break agreement and renounce the lie that_____."

Take a moment and let the Holy Spirit comfort you and restore you.

Ask the Lord:

"Lord, is there anything You want to give me in return for all the lies I have released to You?"

As you receive them, you can list them here:

Jesus has forgiven all your trespasses and sins. Forgiving yourself is merely coming into agreement with Him.

Forgive yourself out loud:

"Jesus, I come into agreement with You and I completely forgive myself for any way I believed those lies. I release all the lies, and I forgive myself."

Rest here for a moment and enjoy the freedom!

This is where it gets fun. Review the Scriptures again.

> Be renewed in the spirit of your minds, and put on the new self, created after the likeness of God in true righteousness and holiness. – Ephesians 4:23-24

> And I am sure of this, that He who began a good work in you will bring it to completion at the day of Jesus Christ. – Philippians 1:6

Ask the Lord:

"Now that I have renounced the lies and forgiven everyone, what are the promises and truths available to me in those Scriptures?"

List what He reveals to you:

_____

_____

_____

_____

_____

When the LORD restored the fortunes of Zion, we were like those who dream. Then our mouth was filled with laughter, and our tongue with shouts of joy; then they said among the nations, "The LORD has done great things for them." The LORD has done great things for us; we are glad. – Psalm 126:1-3

Let yourself dream and think about these truths and promises. Let the Holy Spirit reveal how they would affect your life if you believed them and lived them. What would your life look like—be like? How could it affect your relationships, attitude, career, family, etc.?

List the effects below:

_____

_____

_____

_____

What are some practical steps you can take to experience this in your life?

_____

_____

_____

Let yourself receive from the Holy Spirit and ask Him to empower you, make these truths and promises more real in your life, and help you fulfill the dreams He has given you.

Thank the Lord out loud:

"Thank You, Lord, for the truth that_____and thank You for the promise(s) of _____. I receive them from You by faith and ask that You empower them through the Holy Spirit in my life."

Before moving on, write down any additional thoughts now that you have had time to pray, dream, and receive from the Lord.

_____

_____

_____

_____

Truly, truly, I say to you, whoever believes in Me will also do the works that I do; and greater works than these will he do, because I am going to the Father. — John 14:12

Review

What words do you remember from Session One through Session Three that describe who God says you are?

_____

_____

_____

_____

IDENTITY

These are some of the ways the Lord describes you, as we learned from this session. This is who the Lord declares that you are:

Made in God's image, after His likeness

Blessed

Very good

Fearfully and wonderfully made

His workmanship

Created in Christ Jesus for good works

A partner in the gospel

A partaker of grace

Filled with the fruit of righteousness

Worthy of His calling

Not in the flesh, but in the Spirit

Loved

Belonging to Him

Having all sufficiency in all things at all times

Abounding in every good work

Filled with the knowledge of His will

Spiritually wise and understanding

Worthy of the Lord

Fully pleasing to Him

Bearing fruit in every good work

Increasing in the knowledge of God

Strengthened with all power

Qualified to share in the inheritance of the saints in light

Equipped with everything good

Pleasing in His sight

A believer

Glorified in Jesus

Eternally comforted

Hopeful through grace

Established in every good work and word

Entrusted

Fruitful

A faithful worker

A laborer of love

Steadfast

Hopeful in our Lord

Not under the law

Loving

Joyful

Peaceful

Patient

Kind

Good

Faithful

Gentle

Self-controlled

Belonging to Christ

A light in the Lord

A child of light

Right

True

Trained by grace to renounce ungodliness

Upright

Godly

Redeemed from all lawlessness

Purified for Him

His people

His possession

Zealous for good works

Justified by His grace

An heir according to the hope of eternal life

Devoted to good works

Review this list of identity descriptions and write down the ones that stand out and inspire you:

_____

_____

_____

_____

Take a moment to pray and reflect on these descriptions and write down a statement of faith of your own:

_____

_____

_____

_____

_____

_____

Declare this over yourself out loud.

Wrap Up

Ask God:

"What is the main thing You want me to learn from this session?"

_____

_____

"How can this affect my life now?"

_____

_____

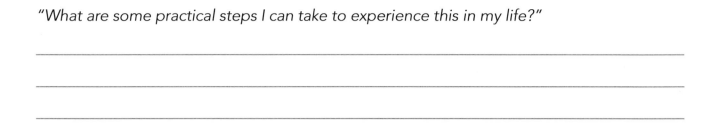

"What are some practical steps I can take to experience this in my life?"

_____

_____

_____

Take a few moments right now and thank God for what He revealed to you.

Practical Take Away Tips

Read through the identity descriptions, memorize them, and declare them over yourself.

Re-read and declare the statements of faith from this session, both the given statements and the one you created for yourself.

Remind yourself of the truths and promises that God revealed to you and continue to dream and ask God to make them more real in your life.

Copy and use the blank Restoration Process on page 165 of the Appendix with the following Scriptures, or any Scriptures that God highlights to you.

- Ephesians 2:10

- Philippians 1:9-11

- 2 Corinthians 9:8

- Colossians 1:11-12

- Philippians 2:13

Session 5

Am I Pure?

CONTENTS

ARE YOU PURE?

Our choices, feelings, behaviors, and overall peace will be affected by what we believe about purity. Lies regarding purity bring shame, guilt, and condemnation into the life of a believer. Freedom in this one area can change our entire outlook on life.

Many followers of Jesus link their perception of their purity to their behavior. Most likely, that is where your mind went as soon as you started this session. For some reason, purity seems to be defined, in the body of Christ, by certain behaviors.

> By this we shall know that we are of the truth and reassure our heart before Him; for whenever our heart condemns us, God is greater than our heart, and He knows everything. Beloved, if our heart does not condemn us, we have confidence before God; and whatever we ask we receive from Him, because we keep His commandments and do what pleases Him. And this is His commandment, that we believe in the name of His Son Jesus Christ and love one another, just as He has commanded us. Whoever keeps His commandments abides in God, and God in Him. And by this we know that He abides in us, by the Spirit whom He has given us. – 1 John 3:19-24

Is there anything we can do to make ourselves pure?

> Who can say, "I have made my heart pure; I am clean from my sin"?
> – Proverbs 20:9

In this session, we will look at our purity in Christ, and discover what that means for us as believers.

Read Titus 2:11-15

Titus 2:14

God gave Himself_____

to redeem us from_____

and to_____

_____

Titus 2:15

Declare these things with all authority._____

_____

God gave Himself, for you, to redeem you from all lawlessness, and purify you for Himself. You are His pure possession. Declare this with all authority and let no one disregard you.

Let's look at the definition of "purify" and then examine the Scripture in light of this definition.

> **Purify** – the Greek word used here is **katharizō** (Strong's G2511)
> It means: to make clean – cleanse – to cleanse by curing – to free from defilement of sin and fault – to purify from wickedness – to free from guilt of sin – to purify – to consecrate by purifying – to consecrate or dedicate – to pronounce clean

An expression of the Scripture including the fullness of that definition could be:

God gave Himself to redeem you, free you from all defilement of sin and fault, purify you from wickedness, set you free from the guilt of sin, consecrate you, pronounce you clean, and dedicate you as His own. Let no one disregard or despise you, including yourself.

Has God Made You Pure?

Read John 15:1-5

John 15:3

You are already_____ because _____

_____

Read 1 Corinthians 5:6-8

1 Corinthians 5:7

Cleanse out the old leaven that you may be a new lump,_____

_____

1 Corinthians 5:8

Let us therefore celebrate the festival, not with the old leaven…but with_____

_____

Read Ephesians 1:3-10

Ephesians 1:4

He chose us in Him before the foundation of the world, that we should be_____

_____

Read Ephesians 5:25-33

Ephesians 5:25

Christ loved the church and_____

Ephesians 5:26

that He might_____

by the washing of water_____

Ephesians 5:27

so that He might present the church to Himself_____

_____

_____

Cleansing out the old leaven is the same as putting off the old self. Be transformed by the renewing of your mind. Cleanse out the old leaven, in the spirit and attitude of your mind, and believe that you are a new lump. For Christ, our Passover lamb, has been sacrificed. You really are the unleavened bread of sincerity and truth.

Read Colossians 1:15-23

Colossians 1:21-22

You, who once were_____

He has now reconciled_____

in order to present you_____

_____

Read Colossians 3:11-12

Colossians 3:12

as God's chosen and elect ones,_____

put on_____

_____

Read Hebrews 13:11-12

Hebrews 13:12

Jesus also suffered outside the gate_____

_____

Let's look at the definitions of "clean," "blameless," and "holy," and then examine the Scripture in light of these definitions.

Clean – the Greek word used here is **katharos** (Strong's G2513)
It means: clean – pure – purified by fire – cleansed by pruning and fitted to bear fruit – freedom from corrupt desire – freedom from sin and guilt – freedom from falsehood – blameless – innocent – unstained from the guilt of anything

Blameless – the Greek word used here is **amōmos** (Strong's G299)
It means: without blemish – a sacrifice without spot or blemish – faultless – unblameable

An expression of the Scripture including the fullness of those definitions could be:

Jesus loves you and gave Himself up for you. He suffered on the cross and sanctified you through His own blood. He chose you in Him to be a most holy saint. You are blameless, faultless, and without blemish. He presents you before Himself as a holy saint. You are already clean, pure, and free from corrupt desires, sin, guilt, and falsehood. You are fitted and ready to bear fruit because of the word He spoke to you and over you.

Consider this...

What are the truths that God is revealing to you personally about these Scriptures?

_____

_____

_____

How could believing these truths affect your life?

_____

_____

_____

What are some practical steps you can take to experience these truths in your life?

_____

_____

_____

Now ask the Holy Spirit to empower you and make these truths more real in your life.

Statement of Faith

I am God's beloved, purified possession. Jesus gave Himself for me so that I could be spotless, without blemish, and free from accusation. He washed me clean, and sanctified me by the word that He spoke to me and over me. He chose me, in Him, to be holy and blameless. I am holy and blameless. I am a dearly loved saint: a guiltless, faultless, clean, and pure saint.

The aim of our charge is love that issues from a pure heart and a good conscience and a sincere faith. – 1 Timothy 1:5

ARE YOU KEPT PURE?

Read 1 Corinthians 1:4-9

1 Corinthians 1:8

Lord Jesus Christ, who will_____

_____

1 Corinthians 1:9

God is faithful, by whom_____

_____

Read Philippians 1:3-11

Philippians 1:6

He who began a good work in you_____

Philippians 1:9

And it is my prayer that your love_____

_____

Philippians 1:10

so that you may approve what is excellent_____

_____

Philippians 1:11

filled with_____

_____

Read 1 Thessalonians 3:11-13

1 Thessalonians 3:12

may the Lord_____

_____

1 Thessalonians 3:13

so that He may establish your hearts_____

_____

at the coming of our Lord_____

Read 1 Thessalonians 5:23-24

1 Thessalonians 5:23

Now may the God of peace Himself_____

and may your whole spirit and soul and body_____

_____

1 Thessalonians 5:24

He who calls you is faithful;_____

Read Jude 24-25

Jude 24

Now to Him who is able_____

and to present you_____

_____

to the only God, our Savior, through Jesus Christ our Lord, be glory, majesty, dominion,

power, and authority,_____

In 1 Corinthians 1:8, the Word tells us that the Lord Jesus Christ will sustain us guiltless.

In 1 Thessalonians 5:23, the Word tells us that we will be kept blameless.

Let's look at the definitions of "sustain" and "kept" and then examine the Scripture in light of these definitions.

> **Sustain** – the Greek word used here is **bebaioō** (Strong's G950)
> It means: to make firm – establish – confirm – make sure
>
> **Kept** – the Greek word used here is **tēreō** (Strong's G5083)
> It means: to attend to carefully – take care of – to guard – to keep one in the state in which he is – to observe – to undergo something

An expression of the Scripture including the fullness of those definitions could be:

Jesus Himself has established you in holiness and purity. He sanctifies you completely. The God of peace Himself will guard, confirm, sustain, and strengthen you. He will keep your whole spirit, soul, and body guiltless and pure. He who calls you is faithful; He will surely do it.

Consider this...

What are the truths that God is revealing to you personally about these Scriptures?

_____

_____

_____

How could believing these truths affect your life?

_____

_____

_____

What are some practical steps you can take to experience these truths in your life?

_____

_____

_____

Now ask the Holy Spirit to empower you and make these truths more real in your life.

Statement of Faith

I was called into fellowship with Jesus. I abound in love, with more and more knowledge and discernment. I am pure, blameless, and filled with the fruit of righteousness. He is completing the good work He started in me, and will sustain me guiltless until the end. The Lord increases my love for all the saints. My heart is established as blameless and holy before God, with all the saints. The God of peace is faithful; He is sanctifying me completely. God is able to keep me from stumbling, and present my whole spirit, soul, and body blameless in His presence.

To the pure, all things are pure. — Titus 1:15a

═══

THE NEW COVENANT

Read Hebrews 9:11-10:25

Hebrews 9:12

He entered once for all into the most holy place, with and by means of_____

_____

having obtained and secured_____

Hebrews 9:14

How much more will the blood of Christ, who through the eternal Spirit offered Himself without spot or blemish to God_____

_____

Hebrews 9:15

Therefore, for this reason, He is the mediator of_____

since a death has occurred that redeems them from the transgressions committed under the first covenant, so that those who are called may receive_____

_____

Hebrews 9:24

For Christ has entered, not into holy places made with hands, which are copies of the true things, but into heaven itself, now_____

_____

Hebrews 9:26b

But now, He has appeared once for all at the end of the ages_____

_____

Hebrews 9:28

Christ, will appear a second time, to_____

_____

Hebrews 10:1a

The law is only_____

_____instead of the true form of these realities

Hebrews 10:4

It is impossible for the blood of bulls and goats_____

Hebrews 10:7

Then I said, Behold,_____

_____

Hebrews 10:9

He does away with the first in order_____

Hebrews 10:10

And by that will_____

through the offering of the body of Jesus Christ_____

Hebrews 10:12

But when Christ had offered for all time a single sacrifice for sins,_____

_____

Hebrews 10:14

For by a single offering He has_____

_____

Hebrews 10:15

And the Holy Spirit also_____

Hebrews 10:16

This is the covenant that_____

I will put My laws_____

and write them_____

Hebrews 10:17

then He says and adds_____

_____

Hebrews 10:18

Where there is forgiveness of these_____

_____

Hebrews 10:19

Therefore, brothers, we have_____

_____

Hebrews 10:22

Let us draw near with_____

in full_____

with our hearts_____

and our bodies_____

Hebrews 10:23

Let us hold fast _____

_____

for He who promised _____

Let's look at the definition of "perfected" and then examine the Scripture in light of this definition.

> **Perfected** – the Greek word used here is **teleioō** (Strong's G5048)
> It means: to make perfect – to complete – to carry through completely – add what is yet wanting in order to render a thing full – to be found perfect – to bring to the end – to accomplish

An expression of the Scripture including the fullness of that definition could be:

By means of His own blood, Jesus is the mediator of a new covenant. He wrote this covenant on your heart and mind. He has secured your redemption and your promised, eternal inheritance. By His single offering, He has purified your conscience, cleansed your heart, and washed your body. Jesus has completely perfected you, and sanctified you, for all time.

Consider this...

What are the truths that God is revealing to you personally about these Scriptures?

_____

_____

_____

How could believing these truths affect your life?

_____

_____

_____

What are some practical steps you can take to experience these truths in your life?

Now ask the Holy Spirit to empower you and make these truths more real in your life.

Statement of Faith

Jesus has purified my conscience from dead works, and has secured an eternal redemption for me. He mediated a new covenant so that I could receive His promised, eternal inheritance. By the will of God, Jesus' single offering has redeemed me, sanctified me, and perfected me for all time. He appeared on my behalf. His sacrifice put away sin, once for all. God will never again remember my sins and lawless deeds. Jesus has washed my heart and my body clean. He wants me to draw near to Him, with my heart full of the assurance of His faithful promises. God's Word is written on my pure heart and my clean mind. I have confidence to enter the holy places by the blood of Jesus.

> If we walk in the light, as He is in the light, we have fellowship with one another, and the blood of Jesus His Son cleanses us from all sin. – 1 John 1:7

DO YOU HAVE A NEW HEART?

Read Jeremiah 31:31-34

Jeremiah 31:33

I will put My law_____and I will write it_____

And I will be_____and they shall be_____

Jeremiah 31:34

they shall know Me, says the Lord, for I will _____

_____

Read Ezekiel 11:19–20

Ezekiel 11:19

I will give them _____

I will remove _____

and give them _____

Ezekiel 11:20

that they may _____

and _____

they shall be _____ and I will be _____

Read Ezekiel 36:22-29

Ezekiel 36:25

I will sprinkle clean water on you _____

_____

I will cleanse you from _____

Ezekiel 36:26

And I will give you _____

And I will remove _____

and give you _____

Ezekiel 36:27

And I will put _____ and I will

_____ to walk and obey My statutes and carefully obey them.

Read Hebrews 8:7-13

Hebrews 8:10

I will put My laws _____ and write them _____

and I will be _____ and they shall be _____

Read Hebrews 10:11-18

Hebrews 10:14

For by a single offering He has_____

those who are_____

Hebrews 10:15

And the Holy Spirit also_____

Hebrews 10:16

This is the covenant that_____

I will put My laws_____ and _____

Hebrews 10:17

then He says and adds_____

_____

Hebrews 10:18

Where there is forgiveness and remission of these_____

_____

Read 2 Corinthians 3:1-3

2 Corinthians 3:3

You show that you are_____

written not with ink but with_____

not on tablets of stone but_____

In Ezekiel 36:27, the Word tells us that God will cause you to walk in His statutes.

Let's look at the definition of "cause" and then examine the Scripture in light of this definition.

> **Cause** – the Hebrew word used here is ʻasah (Strong's H6213)
> It means: to do – fashion – accomplish – make – to work – produce – to act – effect – to bring about

An expression of the Scripture including the fullness of that definition could be:

God is your God, and you belong to Him. He has cleansed you, given you a new heart, and written His laws on your heart and mind. He has given you His Spirit. His Spirit causes you to walk, do, produce, and effectually accomplish the fulfillment of His statutes. By Jesus' single offering, He has perfected you for all time, and will remember your sins no more.

Consider this...

What are the truths that God is revealing to you personally about these Scriptures?

_____

_____

_____

How could believing these truths affect your life?

_____

_____

_____

What are some practical steps you can take to experience these truths in your life?

_____

_____

_____

Now ask the Holy Spirit to empower you and make these truths more real in your life.

Statement of Faith

God is my God, and I belong to Him. He has cleansed me and removed all my false idols. By Jesus' single offering, He has forgiven all of my sins and will remember them no more. He has removed my old heart of stone, and given me a new heart of flesh. He has written His laws on my mind and my heart. Jesus has given me a new spirit and has perfected me for all time. His Holy Spirit empowers me to walk in His statutes. I am a letter from Christ, written with the Spirit of the living God, on the tablet of my heart.

Truly God is good to Israel, to those who are pure in heart. – Psalm 73:1

What Has God Done For You?

- *He has given Himself up for you.*

- *He has condemned sin in your flesh.*

- *He has removed your old heart of stone.*

- *He has cleansed your conscience from dead works.*

- *He has redeemed you and purified you as His own.*

- *He has made you a new creation alive together with Christ.*

- *He has given you a new heart and a new spirit.*

- *He has put His laws in your heart and in your mind.*

- *He has fulfilled the righteous requirements of the law for you and in you.*

- *He has filled you with the fruit of righteousness.*

- *He has sanctified you and made you holy, blameless, righteous, clean, and pure.*

- *He has secured an eternal redemption for you.*

What Is God Doing For You?

- *He is sustaining you guiltless until the end.*

- *He is completing the good work He started in you.*

- *He is causing you to walk in His statutes.*

- *He is increasing you more and more with knowledge and discernment.*

- *He is making you increase and abound in love for one another.*

- *He is establishing your heart holy and blameless before Him.*

- *He is sanctifying you completely.*

- *He is keeping your spirit, soul, and body blameless.*

OLD COVENANT		NEW COVENANT
Heart of stone	▶ ▶ ▷ ▷	Heart of flesh
Wicked heart	▶ ▶ ▷ ▷	Pure heart
Laws written in stone	▶ ▶ ▷ ▷	Law written on your heart
Sinner trying to follow the righteous requirements of the law	▶ ▶ ▷ ▷	Saint with the righteous requirements of the law fulfilled in your heart
Old Heart	▶ ▶ ▷ ▷	New Heart

Ephesians 4:17-24 teaches:

- You must no longer walk as the Gentiles do, in the futility of their minds.

- That is not the way you learned Christ!

- Put off your old self, which belongs to your former manner of life.

- Be renewed in the spirit of your minds and put on the new self.

- You were created in the likeness of God in true righteousness and holiness.

Let us hold fast the confession of our hope without wavering. By Jesus' single offering, we have been perfected and sanctified for all time. There is no longer any offering for sin. We have confidence to enter the Most Holy Place by the blood of Jesus. God has removed our old heart of stone and given us a new heart that is sincere, clean, pure, and true. The righteous requirements of the law are fulfilled and written on our hearts. We can declare this with all authority. We need not let anyone disregard or despise us, including ourselves.

Finally, brothers, whatever is true, whatever is honorable, whatever is just, whatever is pure, whatever is lovely, whatever is commendable, if there is any excellence, if there is anything worthy of praise, think about these things. – Philippians 4:8

THE RESTORATION PROCESS

The life we live now, we live by faith. A simple definition of faith is:

Believing and living the truth of God's Word, through the power of the Holy Spirit.

With that understanding of faith, let's process through the following Scripture and see what the Lord reveals to you.

Jesus Christ, who gave Himself for us to redeem us from all lawlessness and to purify for Himself a people for His own possession who are zealous for good works. Declare these things; exhort and rebuke with all authority. Let no one disregard you. – Titus 2:14-15

Take a moment to pray and invite God to meet with you in this process. Reflect on Titus 2:14-15, and ask the Holy Spirit to reveal the truth of what God is saying in that Scripture.

List the truth that was revealed to you:

_____

_____

_____

_____

_____

Review Titus 2:14-15 one more time and ask the Lord to reveal any of your thoughts or feelings that may be opposed to that Scripture.

Ask the Lord what lies you are believing that are connected to those thoughts and feelings.

List the lies that were revealed:

_____

_____

_____

_____

Remember to draw near to God and stay aware that He is present with you. As you review this list, ask the Lord if there is anyone you need to forgive that may have taught you these lies or hurt you with these lies. Remember, forgiveness is not about accusation or understanding why someone did what they did; it is about releasing through the blood of Jesus.

As the Lord leads, express the forgiveness out loud.

Remember to forgive and release through the blood of Jesus by the power of the Holy Spirit.

"In Jesus' name, I choose to forgive _____ for 'teaching me' or 'hurting me' with the lie that_____."

Now that you have forgiven, you can deal with the lies themselves. Since God revealed to you that these are lies, you can repent from believing the lies by breaking agreement and renouncing them out loud.

"In Jesus' name, I break agreement and renounce the lie that_____."

Take a moment and let the Holy Spirit comfort you and restore you.

Ask the Lord:

"Lord, is there anything You want to give me in return for all the lies I have released to You?"

As you receive them, you can list them here:

_____

_____

_____

Jesus has forgiven all your trespasses and sins. Forgiving yourself is merely coming into agreement with Him.

Forgive yourself out loud:

"Jesus, I come into agreement with You and I completely forgive myself for any way I believed those lies. I release all the lies, and I forgive myself."

Rest here for a moment and enjoy the freedom!

This is where it gets fun. Review the Scripture again.

Jesus Christ, who gave Himself for us to redeem us from all lawlessness and to purify for Himself a people for His own possession who are zealous for good works. Declare these things; exhort and rebuke with all authority. Let no one disregard you. – Titus 2:14-15

Ask the Lord:

"Now that I have renounced the lies and forgiven everyone, what are the promises and truths available to me in that Scripture?"

List what He reveals to you:

_____

_____

_____

_____

_____

When the LORD restored the fortunes of Zion, we were like those who dream. Then our mouth was filled with laughter, and our tongue with shouts of joy; then they said among the nations, "The LORD has done great things for them." The LORD has done great things for us; we are glad. – Psalm 126:1-3

Let yourself dream and think about these truths and promises. Let the Holy Spirit reveal how they would affect your life if you believed them and lived them. What would your life look like—be like? How could it affect your relationships, attitude, career, family, etc.?

List the effects below:

_____

_____

_____

_____

What are some practical steps you can take to experience this in your life?

_____

_____

_____

Let yourself receive from the Holy Spirit and ask Him to empower you, make these truths and promises more real in your life, and help you fulfill the dreams He has given you.

Thank the Lord out loud:

"Thank You, Lord, for the truth that _____ and thank You for the promise(s) of _____. I receive them from You by faith and ask that You empower them through the Holy Spirit in my life."

Before moving on, write down any additional thoughts now that you have had time to pray, dream, and receive from the Lord.

_____

_____

_____

Review

What words do you remember from Session One through Session Four that describe who God says you are?

_____

_____

_____

_____

IDENTITY

These are some of the ways the Lord describes you, as we learned from this session. This is who the Lord declares that you are:

Of the truth

Confident before God

Pleasing to Him

Redeemed from all lawlessness

Purified for Him

His people

His own possession

Zealous for good works

Clean

Unleavened

Sincere

True

Chosen in Him

Holy

Blameless

Loved

Sanctified

Presented in splendor

Without spot or wrinkle

Without blemish

Reconciled

One of God's chosen

Beloved

Compassionate

Kind

Humble

Meek

Patient

Sanctified through Jesus' own blood

Guiltless

Called into the fellowship of His Son

A letter from Christ written with the Spirit of the living God

Pure

Abounding in love

Filled with the fruit of righteousness

Abounding in knowledge and discernment

A saint

Eternally redeemed

Pure in conscience

A servant of the living God

Perfected for all time

True hearted

Clean hearted

Clean in conscience

Washed with pure water

Cleansed from all sin

God's people

Cleansed from all uncleanliness

Cleansed by the washing of water with the Word

Review this list of identity descriptions and write down the ones that stand out and inspire you:

_____

_____

_____

_____

Take a moment to pray and reflect on these descriptions and write down a statement of faith of your own:

_____

_____

_____

_____

_____

Declare this over yourself out loud.

Wrap Up

Ask God:

"What is the main thing You want me to learn from this session?"

_____

_____

"How can this affect my life now?"

_____

_____

"What are some practical steps I can take to experience this in my life?"

_____

_____

_____

Take a few moments right now and thank God for what He revealed to you.

Practical Take Away Tips

Read through the identity descriptions, memorize them, and declare them over yourself.

Re-read and declare the statements of faith from this session, both the given statements and the one you created for yourself.

Remind yourself of the truths and promises that God revealed to you. Continue to dream and ask God to make them more real in your life.

Copy and use the blank Restoration Process on page 165 of the Appendix with the following Scriptures, or any Scriptures that God highlights to you.

- John 15:3

- 1 Corinthians 1:5-9

- 1 Thessalonians 5:23-24

- Hebrews 10:14

Session 6

Am I Accepted?

CONTENTS

ARE YOU CHOSEN AND ACCEPTED?

So far, we have looked extensively into our transformation from death to life. We were dead in our sins and our transgressions, alienated from God, and enemies with Him in our minds. Jesus, in His great mercy, died for us while we were yet sinners. He condemned sin in our flesh, so that the righteous requirements of the law could be fulfilled in us. We are alive in Christ, now having the righteousness of God. We are a new creation – redeemed, sanctified, justified, washed clean, and reconciled to God. We are God's workmanship, created in Christ, and alive in the Spirit. He created and established us for good works as worthy partners of grace. We are His wonderful, qualified, and purified possession. We are filled with the fruit of righteousness, and we belong to God as spotless, guiltless, faultless, and sinless saints.

Jesus Christ, the King of Kings, has done all of this for us. He has also prepared a place specifically for us. He is coming back for us, so that we can be with Him right where He is.

> Let not your hearts be troubled. Believe in God; believe also in Me. In My Father's house are many rooms. If it were not so, would I have told you that I go to prepare a place for you? And if I go and prepare a place for you, I will come again and will take you to Myself, that where I am you may be also. – John 14:1-3

Do you believe that you are accepted? The lie that we are not accepted is commonly used by the enemy to keep followers of Jesus from receiving God's love. Believing the truth that we are accepted allows us to receive the love of God.

In this session, we will examine the truth that we are chosen and accepted before God.

Read Acts 10:34-43

Acts 10:34

Then Peter said:_____

_____

Acts 10:35

Anyone who fears Him and does what is right is_____

Acts 10:43

everyone who believes in Him_____

Read Romans 12:1-2

Romans 12:1

Present your bodies as_____

_____

Romans 12:2

Do not be conformed to this world, but_____

_____

that by testing you may_____

_____

Read Romans 14:17-19

Romans 14:17

For the kingdom of God is not a matter of eating and drinking, but of_____

_____

Romans 14:18

Whoever thus serves Christ is_____

Read Romans 15:1-7

Romans 15:7

Therefore_____

as_____for the glory of God.

As we have learned, there is nothing that we can do to make ourselves acceptable to God. It is the single offering of Jesus Christ that has perfected us for all time. We have also learned that coming into agreement with God and presenting ourselves to Him as acceptable is our reasonable, logical, and spiritual act of service and worship. Thank You, Jesus.

Read 1 Thessalonians 1:1-5

1 Thessalonians 1:4

For we know, loved by God,_____

1 Thessalonians 1:5

because our gospel came to you not only in word, but also in_____

_____

Read 1 Peter 2:1-10

1 Peter 2:4

As you come to Him,_____rejected by men

but in the sight of God_____

1 Peter 2:5

you yourselves_____

are being built up as a spiritual house_____

to offer_____

1 Peter 2:6b

whoever believes in Him_____

1 Peter 2:9

But you are_____

_____

that you may proclaim the praises and excellencies of Him who_____

_____

1 Peter 2:10

Once you were not a people, but now you are_____

once you had not received mercy, but now you have_____

In Romans 15:7, the Word tells us that Christ welcomes us. Some translations use the words receive or accept.

In 1 Peter 2:4, the Word tells us that we are precious in the sight of God. Some translations use the word priceless.

Let's look at the definitions of "welcome" and "precious" and then examine the Scripture in light of these definitions.

> **Welcome** – the Greek word used here is **proslambanō** (Strong's G4355)
> It means: to take to – to take to one's self – to take as one's companion – to receive into one's home – to receive – to grant access to one's heart – to take into friendship
>
> **Precious** – the Greek word used here is **entimos** (Strong's G1784)
> It means: held in honor – prized – precious – valuable – of great value or worth

An expression of the Scripture including the fullness of those definitions could be:

You are held in great honor and worth in the sight of God. You are chosen and precious. Christ has received you, taken you to Himself, and granted you access to His heart as a friend. Therefore, receive one another as friends for the glory of God.

Consider this...

What are the truths that God is revealing to you personally about these Scriptures?

....

....

....

How could believing these truths affect your life?

....

....

....

What are some practical steps you can take to experience these truths in your life?

Now ask the Holy Spirit to empower you and make these truths more real in your life.

Statement of Faith

I am chosen by God, and precious in His sight. I am a living sacrifice, holy and acceptable to God. I am able to discern and prove His will. Christ has welcomed me for the glory of God, and I will not be put to shame. My spiritual sacrifices are acceptable to God through Jesus. Like a living stone, I am being built up as a spiritual house to be a holy priest. God loves me and has chosen me to be a royal priest. He called me out of darkness and into His marvelous light. He called me to be His own, and to proclaim His greatness. God is great!

Then man prays to God, and He accepts him; he sees His face with a shout of joy, and He restores to man his righteousness. – Job 33:26

I myself am satisfied about you, my brothers, that you yourselves are full of goodness, filled with all knowledge and able to instruct one another. – Romans 15:14

ARE YOU CALLED AND DO YOU BELONG?

Read Romans 1:1-6

Romans 1:6

including you who are_____

Read Philippians 3:7-16

Philippians 3:11

that I may attain_____

Philippians 3:12b

I press on to_____

for which and because Christ Jesus has_____

Philippians 3:13

I do not consider that I have made it my own. But one thing I do_____

_____

Philippians 3:14

I press on toward the goal for the prize_____

_____

Philippians 3:15a

Let those of us who are mature_____

Do not be conformed to the pattern of this world or allow your past to define you. Be transformed by the renewing of your mind and think in a mature way. Examine, recognize as genuine, and discern that you are good, acceptable, and perfect in Christ.

Read 1 Corinthians 1:4-9

1 Corinthians 1:4

I give thanks to my God always for you because of_____

_____

1 Corinthians 1:5

in every way you were_____

_____

1 Corinthians 1:6

even as the testimony about Christ was_____

1 Corinthians 1:7

so that you are_____as you wait for

the revealing of our Lord Jesus Christ,

1 Corinthians 1:8

who will_____in the day of

our Lord Jesus Christ.

1 Corinthians 1:9

God is faithful, by whom_____

_____

Read Ephesians 1:15-19

Ephesians 1:17

The Father of glory, may give you_____

_____

Ephesians 1:18

Having_____

that you may know what is_____

what are the riches_____

Ephesians 1:19

the immeasurable and incomparable_____

_____

according to the working_____

Read Ephesians 4:1-8

Ephesians 4:1

I therefore, urge you to walk in a manner worthy_____

_____

Ephesians 4:2

with all_____

_____

Ephesians 4:3

Eager to maintain the unity of the Spirit_____

Ephesians 4:4-5

There is_____

just as_____

_____one Lord, one faith, one baptism

Ephesians 4:6

one God and Father _____ who is over all and through all and_____

Let's look at the definitions of "worthy," "called," and "calling," and then examine the Scripture in light of these definitions.

> **Worthy** – the Greek word used here is **axiōs** (Strong's G516)
> It means: suitably – worthy – in a manner worthy of – fitting – corresponding to – properly
>
> **Called** – the Greek word used here is **kaleō** (Strong's G2564)
> It means: to call – to call aloud – to invite – to call by name – to give a name to – to be called
>
> **Calling** – the Greek word used here is **klēsis** (Strong's G2821)
> It means: a calling – calling to – a call – an invitation – the divine invitation of God's salvation

An expression of the Scripture including the fullness of those definitions could be:

God, who is faithful, invited and called you by name into the fellowship of His Son, Jesus Christ our Lord. Therefore, you are encouraged to walk, live, and behave in a manner corresponding to, and properly fitting to, the worth of this personal invitation and calling by name. The Lord Himself has divinely called you.

Consider this...

What are the truths that God is revealing to you personally about these Scriptures?

_____

_____

_____

How could believing these truths affect your life?

_____

_____

_____

What are some practical steps you can take to experience these truths in your life?

_____

_____

_____

Now ask the Holy Spirit to empower you and make these truths more real in your life.

Statement of Faith

God called me, by name, to belong to Jesus Christ. He has made me His own. The testimony of Christ is confirmed in me, and I am not lacking in any gift. In Jesus, I am enriched in all speech and knowledge. God has called me into the fellowship of His Son, and He will sustain me guiltless until the day of our Lord Jesus Christ. The Father of glory has given me the Spirit of wisdom and revelation in the knowledge of Him. Having the eyes of my heart enlightened, I can know the hope to which He has called me. I can know the riches of His glorious inheritance in the saints.

For the gifts and the calling of God are irrevocable. – Romans 11:29

ARE YOU INCLUDED AND SEALED?

Read John 14:1-3

John 14:2

In my Father's house are many rooms. If it were not so, would I have told you_____

_____

John 14:3

And if I go and prepare a place for you,_____

_____, that where I am_____

Read John 17:20-26

John 17:20

I do not pray and ask for these only,_____

_____

John 17:21

that they may all be one, just as You, Father, are in Me, and I in You,_____

_____, so that the world may believe that You sent Me.

John 17:22

The glory that You have given Me I have given to them,_____

_____

John 17:23

_____ and You in Me,_____

so that the world may know that You sent Me_____

_____

John 17:24

Father,_____ , whom You have given Me,

_____ , to see My glory

that You have given Me because You loved Me before the foundation of the world.

John 17:26

I made known to them Your name, and I will continue to make it known, that the love with

with which You have loved Me_____

_____

We are one with God. Jesus gave us His glory so that we can be one, even as He is one with the Father. Jesus is in us, and we are in Jesus, so that we can be perfectly one. The Father loves us even as He loves Jesus.

Read Ephesians 1:11-14

Ephesians 1:11

In Him we have_____

having been_____

Ephesians 1:12

we who hope in Christ_____

Ephesians 1:13

_____when you heard the word of

truth, the gospel of your salvation, and believed in Him,_____

_____

Ephesians 1:14

who is_____

until_____

Read 2 Corinthians 1:12-22

2 Corinthians 1:19

Jesus Christ, whom we preached among you, was not Yes and No, but_____

_____

2 Corinthians 1:20

For all the promises of God_____

2 Corinthians 1:21

And God who_____in Christ

and has_____

2 Corinthians 1:22

God, who has_____

And given us_____

In Ephesians 1:13, the Word tells us that we were sealed with the promised Holy Spirit. In 2 Corinthians 1:22, the Word tells us that God has put His seal on us and given us the promised Holy Spirit.

Let's look at the definition of "seal" and then examine the Scripture in light of this definition.

Seal – the Greek word used here is **sphragizō** (Strong's G4972)
It means: to set a seal upon – mark with a seal – to seal for security – to hide – keep secret – to prove – to confirm – attest to – authenticate – place beyond doubt

An expression of the Scripture including the fullness of that definition could be:

God, who establishes you in Christ, has anointed you and set His seal of security on you. He has proven you, marked you, and given you His Spirit in your heart as a guarantee. When you believed in Jesus Christ, you were authenticated and confirmed with the promised Holy Spirit, guaranteeing your inheritance.

Consider this...

What are the truths that God is revealing to you personally about these Scriptures?

_____

_____

_____

How could believing these truths affect your life?

_____

_____

_____

What are some practical steps you can take to experience these truths in your life?

_____

_____

_____

Now ask the Holy Spirit to empower you and make these truths more real in your life.

Statement of Faith

Jesus Himself is praying for me. He gave me His glory so that I may be one with Him, just as He is one with the Father. I am one with God. The Father loves me, even as He loves Jesus. Jesus desires me to be with Him where He is. In Him, I have obtained an inheritance according to His purpose. I have been sealed with the promised Holy Spirit, guaranteeing my inheritance. I am established and anointed in Christ. My heart is filled with His Spirit.

If then you have been raised with Christ, seek the things that are above, where Christ is, seated at the right hand of God. Set your minds on things that are above, not on things that are on earth. For you have died, and your life is hidden with Christ in God. When Christ who is your life appears, then you also will appear with Him in glory.
– Colossians 3:1-4

ARE YOU APPROVED AND BLESSED?

Read Romans 4:4-8

Romans 4:6

David also speaks of_____ to whom

God counts righteousness apart from works:

Romans 4:7

_____are those whose lawless deeds are forgiven, and whose

sins are covered;

Romans 4:8

_____is the man against whom the Lord will not count his sin

Read Galatians 3:1-9

Galatians 3:7

Know then that it is those of faith who are_____

Galatians 3:8b

In you shall all the nations_____

Galatians 3:9

those who are of faith_____

Read Ephesians 1:3-7

Ephesians 1:3

Blessed be the God and Father of our Lord Jesus Christ, who has_____

_____

Ephesians 1:4

even as He_____before the foundation of the world,

that we should be_____

Ephesians 1:5

He predestined us for adoption_____

according to_____

Ephesians 1:6

to the praise of His glorious grace, which He has_____

Read 1 Thessalonians 2:1-4

1 Thessalonians 2:4

we have been_____

Read 2 Timothy 2:14-16

2 Timothy 2:15

Do your best to present yourself to God_____

_____rightly handling the word of truth.

In 1 Thessalonians 2:4, the Word tells us that we are approved by God. 2 Timothy 2:15 tells us to present ourselves to Him approved. Two different Greek words are used in these passages to express the word "approved."

Let's look at these definitions of "approved" and then examine the Scripture in light of these definitions.

1 Thessalonians 2:4

> **Approved** – the Greek word used here is **dokimazō** (Strong's G1381)
> It means: to test – examine – prove – scrutinize – to recognize as genuine after examination –
> deem worthy – to approve

2 Timothy 2:15

> **Approved** – the Greek word used here is **dokimos** (Strong's G1384)
> It means: accepted – particularly of coins and money – pleasing – acceptable

An expression of the Scripture including the fullness of those definitions could be:

You have been proven, recognized as genuine, and deemed worthy to be entrusted with the gospel. Do your best to rightly handle the word of truth by presenting yourself to God as who you really are – a pleasing, valuable, approved, and acceptable worker, who has no need to be ashamed.

Consider this...

What are the truths that God is revealing to you personally about these Scriptures?

How could believing these truths affect your life?

What are some practical steps you can take to experience these truths in your life?

_____

_____

_____

Now ask the Holy Spirit to empower you and make these truths more real in your life.

Statement of Faith

I have been blessed and counted righteous, apart from my works. God has forgiven and covered my sins. He will never count them against me. I am blessed along with Abraham as a son/daughter. God, the Father of my Lord Jesus Christ, has blessed me with every spiritual blessing in the heavenly places. He has chosen me, in love, to be holy and blameless before Him as a son/daughter, through Jesus Christ. I am approved, blessed in the beloved, and trusted with the good news of Jesus Christ. I am an approved worker and have no need to be ashamed.

Working together with Him, then, we appeal to you not to receive the grace of God in vain. For He says, "In a favorable time I listened to you, and in a day of salvation I have helped you." Behold, now is the favorable time; behold, now is the day of salvation.
– 2 Corinthians 6:2-3

For you bless the righteous, O Lord; You cover him with favor as with a shield. – Psalm 5:12

LIES AND ACCUSATIONS FROM THE ENEMY		TRUTH AND DECLARATIONS FROM GOD
Unaccepted	▶ ▶ ▷	Accepted
Unwelcome	▶ ▶ ▷	Welcome
Unwanted	▶ ▶ ▷	Chosen
Unknown	▶ ▶ ▷	Included
Not good enough	▶ ▶ ▷	Approved
Worthless	▶ ▶ ▷	Precious
Rejected	▶ ▶ ▷	Called

If we believe the lies of the enemy and reject ourselves, we will reject God's love and not be able to love others.

Accepting the truth of who we are in Christ allows us to receive the love of God and express His love to the world.

THE RESTORATION PROCESS

The life we live now, we live by faith. A simple definition of faith is:

Believing and living the truth of God's Word, through the power of the Holy Spirit.

With that understanding of faith, let's process through the following Scripture and see what the Lord reveals to you.

I myself am satisfied about you, my brothers, that you yourselves are full of goodness, filled with all knowledge and able to instruct one another. – Romans 15:14

Take a moment to pray and invite God to meet with you in this process. Reflect on Romans 15:14, and ask the Holy Spirit to reveal the truth of what God is saying in that Scripture.

List the truth that was revealed to you:

_____

_____

_____

_____

Review Romans 15:14 one more time and ask the Lord to reveal any of your thoughts or feelings that may be opposed to that Scripture.

Ask the Lord what lies you believe that are connected to those thoughts and feelings.

List the lies that were revealed:

_____

_____

_____

_____

Remember to draw near to God and stay aware that He is present with you. As you review this list, ask the Lord if there is anyone you need to forgive that may have taught you these lies or hurt you with these lies. Remember, forgiveness is not about accusation or understanding why someone did what they did; it is about releasing through the blood of Jesus.

As the Lord leads, express the forgiveness out loud.

Remember to forgive and release through the blood of Jesus by the power of the Holy Spirit.

"In Jesus' name, I choose to forgive _____ for 'teaching me' or 'hurting me' with the lie that _____ ."

Now that you have forgiven, you can deal with the lies themselves. Since God revealed to you that these are lies, you can repent from believing the lies by breaking agreement and renouncing them out loud.

"In Jesus' name, I break agreement and renounce the lie that_____."

Take a moment and let the Holy Spirit comfort you and restore you.

Ask the Lord:

"Lord, is there anything You want to give me in return for all the lies I have released to You?"

As you receive them, you can list them here:

_____

_____

_____

Jesus has forgiven all your trespasses and sins. Forgiving yourself is merely coming into agreement with Him.

Forgive yourself out loud:

"Jesus, I come into agreement with You and I completely forgive myself for any way I believed those lies. I release all the lies, and I forgive myself."

Rest here for a moment and enjoy the freedom!

This is where it gets fun. Review the Scripture again.

> I myself am satisfied about you, my brothers, that you yourselves are full of goodness, filled with all knowledge and able to instruct one another. – Romans 15:14

Ask the Lord:

"Now that I have renounced the lies and forgiven everyone, what are the promises and truths available to me in that Scripture?"

List what He reveals to you:

_____

_____

_____

_____

_____

> When the LORD restored the fortunes of Zion, we were like those who
> dream. Then our mouth was filled with laughter, and our tongue with
> shouts of joy; then they said among the nations, "The LORD has done
> great things for them." The LORD has done great things for us; we
> are glad. – Psalm 126:1-3

Let yourself dream and think about these truths and promises. Let the Holy Spirit reveal how they would affect your life if you believed them and lived them. What would your life look like—be like? How could it affect your relationships, attitude, career, family, etc.?

List the effects below:

_____

_____

_____

_____

What are some practical steps you can take to experience this in your life?

_____

_____

_____

Let yourself receive from the Holy Spirit and ask Him to empower you, make these truths and promises more real in your life, and help you fulfill the dreams He has given you.

Thank the Lord out loud:

"Thank You, Lord, for the truth that _____ and thank You for the promise(s) of _____. I receive them from You by faith and ask that You empower them through the Holy Spirit in my life."

Before moving on, write down any additional thoughts now that you have had time to pray, dream, and receive from the Lord.

_____

_____

_____

Review

What words do you remember from Session One through Session Five that describe who God says you are?

_____

_____

_____

_____

IDENTITY

These are some of the ways the Lord describes you, as we learned from this session. This is who the Lord declares that you are:

Acceptable to Him

A living sacrifice

Holy

Acceptable to God

Transformed

Approved by men

Welcome

A brother/sister

Loved by God

Chosen

A living stone

A holy priest

Acceptable

A chosen race

A royal priest

A holy nation

His own possession

Called out of darkness

Called into His marvelous light

God's people

Restored

Righteous

Included

Called to belong to Jesus

Given grace in Christ Jesus

Not lacking any gift

Enriched in Him in all speech and all knowledge

Sustained guiltless

Called into the fellowship of His Son

Given the Spirit of wisdom and revelation in the knowledge of Him

Enlightened to hope

A saint

Humble

Gentle

Patient

Loving

Unified in the Spirit

Peaceful

Called to hope

Irrevocably gifted

Irrevocably called

One with God

Given glory

Loved

An heir of His inheritance

Predestined according to His purpose

The praise of His glory

Established in Christ

Anointed

Sealed

Raised with Christ

Hidden with Christ in God

In glory

Sealed with the promised Holy Spirit

Counted righteous apart from my works

Blessed

Forgiven

Covered

A son/daughter of Abraham

Blessed in Christ with every spiritual blessing in the heavenly places

Chosen in Him

Holy and blameless before Him in love

Predestined for adoption as a son/daughter through Jesus Christ

Blessed in the beloved

Approved by God

Entrusted with the gospel

Approved

A worker that has no need to be ashamed

Favored

Helped by God

Review this list of identity descriptions and write down the ones that stand out and inspire you:

_____

_____

_____

_____

Take a moment to pray and reflect on these descriptions and write down a statement of faith of your own:

_____

_____

_____

_____

_____

Declare this truth over yourself out loud.

Wrap Up

Ask God:

"What is the main thing You want me to learn from this session?"

_____

_____

"How can this affect my life now?"

_____

_____

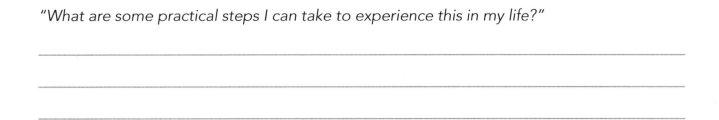

"What are some practical steps I can take to experience this in my life?"

_____

_____

_____

Take a few moments right now and thank God for what He revealed to you.

Practical Take Away Tips

Read through the identity descriptions, memorize them, and declare them over yourself.

Re-read and declare the statements of faith from this session, both the given statements and the one you created for yourself.

Remind yourself of the truths and promises that God revealed to you. Continue to dream and ask God to make them more real in your life.

Copy and use the blank Restoration Process on page 165 of the Appendix with the following Scriptures, or any Scriptures that God highlights to you.

- 1 Corinthians 1:7-9

- John 17:21-24

- Ephesians 1:3-4

- 1 Thessalonians 2:4

CONCLUSION

In this volume, we discovered our redeemed, alive, righteous, fruitful, pure, and accepted identity in Christ. In Volume Two, we will examine our loved, known, trusted, pleasing, powerful, and purposeful identity in Christ.

May God bless you on this journey as you continue to discover who you really are in Him.

APPENDIX

IDENTITY

A believer

A brother/sister

A child of light

A chosen race

A dwelling place for God

A faithful worker

A fellow citizen

A holy nation

A holy priest

A holy temple in the Lord

A laborer of love

A letter from Christ written with the Spirit of the Living God

A light in the Lord

A living sacrifice

A living stone

A member of God's household

A minister of reconciliation

A new creation

A partaker of grace

A partner in the gospel

A peacemaker

A pure virgin to Christ

A royal priest

A saint

A servant of the living God

A slave of God

A slave to righteousness

A son/daughter of Abraham

A worker that has no need to be ashamed

Abounding in every good work

Abounding in knowledge and discernment

Abounding in love

Above reproach before Him

Abraham's offspring

Acceptable

Acceptable to God

Acceptable to Him

Alive in the Spirit

Alive through His Spirit that dwells in me

Alive to God

Alive to God in Christ Jesus

Alive together with Christ

Alive with Christ

An approved worker

An heir according to the hope of eternal life

An heir of His inheritance

An instrument for righteousness

An oak of righteousness

An obedient child

Anointed

Approved

Approved by God

Approved by men

Baptized into Christ Jesus

Bearing fruit in every good work

Belonging to Christ

Belonging to Him

Beloved

Betrothed

Blameless

Blessed

Blessed in Christ with every spiritual blessing in the heavenly places

Blessed in the beloved

Born again of imperishable seed

Brought from death to life

Brought near

Brought to God

Called

Called into His marvelous light

Called into the fellowship of His Son

Called out of darkness

Called to belong to Jesus

Called to hope

Chosen

Chosen in Him

Clean

Clean because of Jesus' Word

Clean hearted

Clean in conscience

Cleansed by the washing of water with the Word

Cleansed from all sin

Cleansed from all uncleanliness

Compassionate

Confident before God

Counted righteous apart from my works

Covered

Created after the likeness of God

Created in Christ

Created in Christ Jesus for good works

Created in true holiness

Created in true righteousness

Crucified with Christ

Crucified with Him

Dead in the flesh

Dead to sin

Dead to the law

Dead to the spirits of the world

Devoted to good works

Enlightened to hope

Enriched in Him in all speech and all knowledge

Entrusted

Entrusted with the gospel

Equipped with everything good

Established in Christ

Established in every good work and word

Eternally comforted

Eternally redeemed

Eternally secure

Faithful

Favored

Fearfully and wonderfully made

Filled with the fruit of righteousness

Filled with the knowledge of His will

Filled with the Spirit

Forgiven

Free

Free from the law of sin and death

Fruitful

Fully pleasing to Him

Gentle

Given glory

Given grace in Christ Jesus

Given the Spirit of wisdom and revelation in the knowledge of Him

Glorified in Jesus

God's people

Godly

Good

Greatly loved

Guiltless

Having all sufficiency in all things at all times

Helped by God

Hidden with Christ in God

His own possession

His people

His possession

His workmanship

Holy

Holy and blameless before Him in love

Hopeful in our Lord

Hopeful through grace

Humble

In Christ

In Christ Jesus

In glory

Included

Increasing in the knowledge of God

Irrevocably called

Irrevocably gifted

Joyful

Justified

Justified apart from works

Justified by faith

Justified by His blood

Justified by His grace

Kind

Loved

Loved by God

Loving

Made in God's image, after His likeness

Meek

New

Not in the flesh, but in the Spirit

Not lacking any gift

Not under the law

Obedient from the heart

Of the truth

One of God's chosen

One with God

Patient

Peaceful

Perfected for all time

Pleasing in His sight

Pleasing to Him

Predestined according to His purpose

Predestined for adoption as a son/daughter through Jesus Christ

Presented in splendor

Pure

Pure in conscience

Purified

Purified for Him

Qualified to share in the inheritance of the saints in light

Raised up with Him

Raised with Christ

Reconciled

Reconciled as one in peace

Reconciled to God

Redeemed

Redeemed from all lawlessness

Redeemed from the curse

Regenerated

Reigning in life

Renewed

Renewed in knowledge after the image of my Creator

Restored

Right

Righteous

Sanctified

Sanctified completely

Sanctified in truth

Sanctified through Jesus' own blood

Sanctified through the offering of Jesus Christ

Saved

Saved by Him

Saved through faith

Sealed

Sealed with the promised Holy Spirit

Seated in heavenly places

Self-controlled

Set free

Set free from sin

Set free in Christ Jesus

Sincere

Spiritually wise and understanding

Steadfast

Strengthened with all power

Sustained guiltless

The praise of His glory

The righteousness of faith

The righteousness of God

Trained by grace to renounce ungodliness

Transformed

True

True hearted

Unashamed

Unified in the Spirit

United with Him in resurrection

Unleavened

Upright

Very good

Washed

Washed with pure water

Welcome

Without blemish

Without spot or wrinkle

Worthy of His calling

Worthy of the Lord

Zealous for good works

THE RESTORATION PROCESS

The life we live now, we live by faith. A simple definition of faith is:

Believing and living the truth of God's Word, through the power of the Holy Spirit.

With that understanding of faith, let's process through the following Scripture and see what the Lord reveals to you.

Write the Scripture here:

_____

_____

_____

_____

Take a moment to pray and invite God to meet with you in this process. Reflect on the Scripture, and ask the Holy Spirit to reveal the truth of what God is saying in that Scripture.

List the truth that was revealed to you:

_____

_____

_____

_____

_____

Review the Scripture one more time and ask the Lord to reveal any of your thoughts or feelings that may be opposed to that Scripture.

Ask the Lord what lies you are believing that are connected to those thoughts and feelings.

List the lies that were revealed:

_____

_____

_____

_____

Remember to draw near to God and stay aware that He is present with you. As you review this list, ask the Lord if there is anyone you need to forgive that may have taught you these lies or hurt you with these lies. Remember, forgiveness is not about accusation or understanding why someone did what they did; it is about releasing through the blood of Jesus.

As the Lord leads, express the forgiveness out loud.

Remember to forgive and release through the blood of Jesus by the power of the Holy Spirit.

"In Jesus' name, I choose to forgive _____ for 'teaching me' or 'hurting me' with the lie that _____ ."

Now that you have forgiven, you can deal with the lies themselves. Since God revealed to you that these are lies, you can repent from believing the lies by breaking agreement and renouncing them out loud.

"In Jesus' name, I break agreement and renounce the lie that_____ ."

Take a moment and let the Holy Spirit comfort you and restore you.

Ask the Lord:

"Lord, is there anything You want to give me in return for all the lies I have released to You?"

As you receive them, you can list them here:

_____

_____

_____

Jesus has forgiven all your trespasses and sins. Forgiving yourself is merely coming into agreement with Him.

Forgive yourself out loud:

"Jesus, I come into agreement with You and I completely forgive myself for any way I believed those lies. I release all the lies, and I forgive myself."

Rest here for a moment and enjoy the freedom!

This is where it gets fun. Review the Scripture again.

Write the Scripture here:

_____

_____

_____

_____

Ask the Lord:

"Now that I have renounced the lies and forgiven everyone, what are the promises and truths available to me in that Scripture?"

List what He reveals to you:

_____

_____

_____

_____

_____

When the LORD restored the fortunes of Zion, we were like those who dream. Then our mouth was filled with laughter, and our tongue with shouts of joy; then they said among the nations, "The LORD has done great things for them." The LORD has done great things for us; we are glad. – Psalm 126:1-3

Let yourself dream and think about these truths and promises. Let the Holy Spirit reveal how they would affect your life if you believed them and lived them. What would your life look like—be like? How could it affect your relationships, attitude, career, family, etc.?

List the effects below:

_____

_____

_____

_____

What are some practical steps you can take to experience this in your life?

_____

_____

_____

Let yourself receive from the Holy Spirit and ask Him to empower you, make these truths and promises more real in your life, and help you fulfill the dreams He has given you.

Thank the Lord out loud:

"Thank You, Lord, for the truth that _____ and thank You for the promise(s) of _____. I receive them from You by faith and ask that You empower them through the Holy Spirit in my life."

Before moving on, write down any additional thoughts now that you have had time to pray, dream, and receive from the Lord.

_____

_____

_____